BRUNSWICK STEW

Joel Haynor (signature)

BRUNSWICK STEW
A VIRGINIA TRADITION

Joseph R. Haynes

AMERICAN PALATE

Published by American Palate
A Division of The History Press
Charleston, SC
www.historypress.net

Copyright © 2017 by Joseph R. Haynes
All rights reserved

Cover image of woman holding the can of stew courtesy of Isle of Wight County Museum. All images herein provided courtesy of the Isle of Wight County Museum are used by permission.

First published 2017

Manufactured in the United States

ISBN 9781625859648

Library of Congress Control Number: 2017944970

Notice: The information in this book is true and complete to the best of our knowledge. It is offered without guarantee on the part of the author or The History Press. The author and The History Press disclaim all liability in connection with the use of this book.

All rights reserved. No part of this book may be reproduced or transmitted in any form whatsoever without prior written permission from the publisher except in the case of brief quotations embodied in critical articles and reviews.

To Gail—my high school sweetheart, my wife, the mother of my children and my best friend.

To Mom and Dad—they taught me the value of honesty, gratitude, compassion, generosity, perseverance and hard work.

CONTENTS

Foreword, by Dr. L. Daniel Mouer	9
Acknowledgements	11
Introduction	13
1. The Barbecue Stews	15
2. Virginia's Food Traditions	26
3. Squirrel Soup	48
4. Barbecue Hash	61
5. Brunswick Stew	77
6. Burgoo	119
7. Recipes	147
Notes	157
Index	183
About the Author	189

FOREWORD

It has been a bit over three years ago that I received an e-mail from a stranger named Joe Haynes. Joe told me he was writing a book about barbecue in Virginia. He had stumbled on some of my writings about influences and interactions between early Virginia settlers and the native Powhatan people of eastern Virginia. He was looking for some clarifications and information. We clearly shared interests in the foodways history of the Old Dominion. Soon I was reading manuscript chapters, and the more I learned about Joe and his project, the more interested I became.

I confess that I was at first wary of becoming too involved. Barbecue can be a passion, and it was clear to me that he was obsessed. He is, I soon learned, a competitive pit master. A big part of his passion was, as one might expect, praising his own home state's barbecue traditions and asserting that Virginia rightly holds pride of place among those claiming to be the historical and cultural source of Southern USA barbecue in all its glorious (and contentious) diversity. That way lies danger, I thought. Will this be another boastful "my barbecue is better than yours" book? Will it turn out to be mainly a cookbook or yet another treatise on a pit master's mysterious techniques and secret ingredients?

In a little over a year, Joe announced that his first book was finished and at the publisher. Soon I had a completed copy in my hand, and I was beyond amazed at his masterful accomplishment. Joe Haynes had demonstrated clearly that his interest far exceeds the scope of most published writing about barbecue in that his research was thorough, scholarly, thoughtful and

Foreword

wonderfully insightful. I quickly recommended Joe's *Virginia Barbecue: A History* to my longtime foodways-scholarship colleagues.

As soon as his book hit the shelves, Joe told me he was already working on his next magnum opus. He was going to tackle Brunswick stew! And tackle it he has, along with barbecue hash, fish frys, Kentucky burgoo and hoecakes. These signature southern dishes belong to the barbecue tradition, which, together with his previous book, Joe thoroughly reveals, explicates and glorifies. He also includes some recipes. Some are his own or his family's, but there are a number from important historic and contemporary stewmasters. That said, these recipes are just a touch of extra frosting on the cake. This is not specifically a recipe book, nor is it a "how to," but you could surely do well if you wanted to use information here to try your hand at a Brunswick stew party.

Joe's work is significant scholarship. This is American culinary history and ethnology at its finest, researched with passion and recited with love, humor and intelligence. Joe understands and appreciates the historical depth and cultural significance of these traditions. He clearly sees and helps tease out the contributions of ancient English foodways and their adaptations to and adoptions of those of Native America, as well as the role of enslaved Africans and African Americans who often were the true masters of the barbecue and stewpot. He follows traditions as they spread and evolved through the southward and westward expansion of the nation.

I cannot imagine reading this book without experiencing a craving in the belly and a mouthwatering wish to relive some of this rich history. So, my friends, read on and learn and be prepared to hunger for a day we can all sit together at a long plank table under green trees near a cool spring and drink cider and eat thick Brunswick stew that has been stirred in an iron washpot for a day or two at an old-fashioned Virginia barbecue. When you've finished this volume, run right out and get a copy of *Virginia Barbecue: A History* if you don't already have it.

L. Daniel Mouer, PhD

ACKNOWLEDGEMENTS

I owe heartfelt thanks to the following people for their invaluable assistance in producing this book:

Josephine Denny
Andrew McCrea
Norman Rainock
Lorraine I. Quillon
Chiles Cridlin
Lucy Tonacci
Alfonso McNeill
Melissa Wuske
Tracy Neikirk at the Ilse of Wight County Museum
Julie and Matt Shaffer at Shaffer's BBQ & Market
Craig Hartman at the Barbeque Exchange
Sandra L. Oliver
Dr. L. Daniel Mouer
Dr. Charlette Woolridge
Diane Dallmeyer at the Chesterfield Historical Society of Virginia
Nancy Richey at the Western Kentucky University Library
Kat Hagedorn, Lawrence Wentzel and Lara Ungar at the University of Michigan Library
Sarah Dorpinghaus at the University of Kentucky Library
Ron Sonntag at Boone Brands

Acknowledgements

Jamestown-Yorktown Foundation

Deborah Padgett and the good people of the re-created Powhatan Indian village at Jamestown Settlement living-history museum, Williamsburg, Virginia

Special thanks to my wife, Gail, for her loving support. Thanks to my parents, who raised me in rural Virginia and instilled in me a love for the food traditions that Virginians have practiced for centuries. Thanks to so many others who helped me complete this book. Unfortunately, I can't name everyone, and my failure to include deserved recognition is not intentional.

INTRODUCTION

Living in central Virginia my whole life, I have seen many changes over the years. We used to have front "poaches" (porches) and back "dōz" (doors). Our midday meal was called "dinner" and our late meal "supper." We ate "pea-can" pie and drank soft drinks that we called "cokes" regardless of the brand or flavor. We knew the difference between grilling and barbecuing and never made the mistake of calling our "charcoal grill" a barbecue grill. We dug potatoes, shelled beans, put wood in the stove on cold mornings, churned butter, plowed the field, shucked corn with a hand-cranked sheller, worked all morning in a field filling bags with "creese" salad (watercress), gleaned corn from fields to feed the hogs and hung hams and bacon in the smokehouse.

My mother used to make Brunswick stew using corn, tomatoes and butterbeans that my father grew. My parents preferred the stew with just fatback or a couple of pork spare ribs in it and no other meats. Being a hunter, my father occasionally made squirrel soup. However, my mother's squirrel gravy was the true squirrel delicacy in our home. She cut the squirrels into quarters and simmered them for a few hours until they were tender. Next, she dredged the squirrel quarters in seasoned flour and fried them. Using the drippings and broth, she made a rich squirrel gravy that she served with hot hoecakes or biscuits. There are few things as delicious as hot hoecakes smothered in gravy made from a Virginia gray squirrel that has spent its whole life dining on whatever it can forage in the deep forest.

Introduction

I never really thought much about growing up in rural Virginia when I was younger. It seemed as if things would always be the same. However, as I grew older, many of the most important people in my family circle passed on. I realized that many of the things I took for granted were passing away with them. I miss every one of them and think of them often. The one thing that brings back my most vivid memories is food. I never smell bacon without thinking of my father's smokehouse. I never eat hoecake or fried chicken without thinking of my mother toiling in the kitchen. Watermelon reminds me of spending time with family and friends on a long, hot summer day. Steamed crabs remind me of my siblings.

I have no desire to return to the past, and I don't think of it as a simpler time. Nevertheless, I now know that preserving the best things from the past can give us a richer present and a happier future. As the apostle Paul wrote, "Prove all things; hold fast that which is good." Virginia's food traditions fall into the "good" category. They are a reminder to Virginians of who we are and where we came from. They reflect the diversity of Virginia's population throughout the centuries and transcend race, religion, politics and class.

This book isn't as much about the past as it is about the future. After all, everyone has to eat. I know of no better way to preserve the best parts of Virginia's long-held food traditions for future generations than by gathering with family and friends from time to time to cook and enjoy a delicious kettle of Virginia-style Brunswick stew.

This book is meant to promote and preserve Virginia's culturally significant Brunswick stew tradition in an entertaining and informative way by:

- Providing a record of the legend, lore and true history (as best as it can be understood) of the barbecue stews
- Providing a record of Virginian food traditions and, to some extent, southern food traditions
- Promoting and preserving authentic Virginia-style Brunswick stew recipes
- Sharing proper and authentic techniques for cooking barbecue stews

Chapter 1
THE BARBECUE STEWS

In the mean time, over a fire was a huge pot, in which had been put water, were placed squirrels—if obtainable—if not, chickens—a piece of bacon, "streak o'fat & streak o'lean," several pounds of butter—tomatoes—butter beans—potatoes—ochra—green corn—Worchester sauce ad libitum—a few pods of red pepper—& salt & pepper: This was allowed to simmer slowly & by the time the [barbecued] *meat was ready—it was ready also. I have eaten many famous ragouts & stews—at the great restaurants in England & on the Continent, but never at Spiers & Ponds or Simpsons—never at Vefours or Voisins—Foyots—or Boeuf à la Mode, have I eaten as divine a concoction as the "Barbecue Stew" made after my Father's receipt. The only difficulty was, that you were tempted to eat so much of it, that it took away your appetite for the delicious barbecued meat.*
—R.T.W. Duke Jr., Recollections *(courtesy University of Virginia, Albert and Shirley Small Special Collections Library)*

In the nineteenth century, friends of lawyer, politician, Confederate veteran and Brunswick stew enthusiast Colonel Richard Thomas Walker Duke Sr. of Albemarle, Virginia, coined the phrase "barbecue stew" to refer to the famous Virginia-style Brunswick stew that he served at old Virginia barbecues hosted on his estate.[1] The barbecue stews aren't necessarily stews made with barbecued meats, although some versions are. Rather, they are stews that are traditionally cooked and served at barbecues and other outdoor feasts in the southern United States. Three of the most famous barbecue stews are Brunswick stew, burgoo and barbecue hash.

Barbecue stew history is full of humor, folksiness and a delightful mixture of fact and myth embodying four hundred years of American history and diversity. People of European, African and Native American ancestry all played an important role in the development of the barbecue stew recipes and the stew stories surrounding them. Each of the stews has served a prominent role in American politics, beginning in the days when politicians stood on tree stumps to deliver speeches at rural community gatherings to modern political rallies in our times.

As the stews spread throughout the country over the last three hundred years, people of each region added their own distinctive touches to the recipes, as well as their own fierce stew loyalty, stew poetry and songs, stew stories, myths and enduring stew legends. Several "stew wars" have been ignited, with various factions claiming their stew recipes to be the true stew, first stew or the best stew. However, no matter the recipe or the regional variation, the stews have served to bring people together from all walks of life, providing the opportunity for rousing entertainment, stimulating conversation, cordial fellowship and warm reunions.

People have been cooking soups and stews for thousands of years. The broth in soup is thin. The broth in stew is rich and thick. The difference between a soup and a stew is particularly important when discussing the barbecue stews. There is no mistaking real Brunswick stew for chicken and vegetable soup, which is what some are trying to pass off as Brunswick stew nowadays. Brunswick stew, like all barbecue stews, must simmer for a long time while being constantly stirred to make it rich, thick and delicious. Sadly, some restaurateurs refuse to invest the time and effort it takes to prepare it properly. Burgoo sometimes suffers a similar fate.

Before the invention of earthen pots, people boiled water in holes or animal skins with hot stones. Consider the Assiniboine people, also known as the Nakota, who were originally from the Northern Great Plains. The name "Assiniboine" means "Stone Boilers" or "those who cook with stones." In order to cook soups and stews in the times before acquiring the knowledge of pottery, the Assiniboines dug a hole in the ground and lined it with the hide of an animal, making a watertight basin. They filled the lined hole with water before adding the soup ingredients. They placed red-hot stones heated in a fire into the water to boil it. They added hot stones as needed to maintain a simmer until the soup was done. Eventually, the Stone Boilers learned to make earthen vessels and later traded with Europeans for metal pots, ultimately giving up the practice of boiling soup with hot stones.

A Virginia Tradition

Delicious Virginia-style Brunswick stew simmering outside in an open cast-iron kettle. Author's collection.

In addition to Native Americans, people all over the world were "stone boilers" in ancient times.[2] The practice of heating water with hot rocks persisted in the United States well into the twentieth century. During the Great Depression, my father's family heated water for scalding hog carcasses in wooden troughs using hot stones and pieces of hot metal, such as old plow points. When scalding hogs, a water temperature of about 165 to 175 degrees Fahrenheit is best, and the hot stones and metal provided sufficient heat to do the job. In times past, Virginians often saved the hair from scalded hogs to use it as a hardening ingredient in the plaster that covered the walls inside their homes. Many renovators have been surprised by this fact when they have demolished walls in old Virginia homes during renovations. Now that's some real Virginia-style rooter-to-the-tooter use of the entire hog.

In seventeenth-century England, pottage was an important food. People put water, grains and, if they were fortunate, meat into a pot and boiled it into a thick gruel. Before serving it to guests, scraps of bread called "sops" topped off the dish. The number of sops in a serving was an indication of the host's generosity.[3] After a little French influence, the word *sops* developed into the English word *soup*.[4] Women in seventeenth-century Africa slow-cooked stews, such as kedjenou (a slow-cooked poultry stew), in earthen pots. African cooks disliked European iron pots because they believed they imparted a bad taste to food.[5]

Long before Europeans stumbled on the Americas, the Algonquian-speaking Powhatan Indians who lived in what is now Virginia had long been practicing the custom of keeping stew simmering in earthen pots set over hot coals at all times of the day and night. Powhatan Indian cooks made soups and stews with ingredients such as corn, beans, squash, fruits, fish and meat. Sometimes they smoked the meat before adding it to the pot.[6] Because they had no set mealtimes, a hot bowl of stew was available whenever someone was hungry. As the Powhatan cooks replenished the pot with ingredients throughout the day, the perpetually simmering pot served to preserve foods by keeping them warm at a safe-to-eat temperature.[7] It was the Powhatan version of our crockpot. The soup or stew simmered "low and slow" for long periods, transforming the ingredients into a delicious, flavorful meal. An Algonquian word for this one-pot meal is *msíckquatash*. The Anglicized version of that word is *succotash*.[8] The combination of corn (maize) with beans used in American recipes was adopted from Native Americans and *msíckquatash* is also an ancestor of Brunswick stew.[9]

Over the first few decades of English settlement in Virginia, the assistance of the Powhatan Indians was very important to the colonists' survival. Many accounts tell of the corn, beans, squash and wild game the Powhatan tribes supplied to colonists when they had no other source of sustenance.[10] A few years ago, archaeologists discovered an early seventeenth-century stew pot made by the Patawomeck tribe (a member of the Powhatan Indian Confederacy) that they traded to Jamestown settlers. The last meal cooked in it was a venison and corn (maize) stew.[11]

In early seventeenth-century Virginia, the uniquely American mix of African, European and Native American cultures and cooking styles made its way to Virginia. Later in the seventeenth century, people of African descent in Virginia began asserting their own culinary contributions. From at least the mid- to late seventeenth century, African influences became more and more prominent.[12] This mixing of food cultures in what is now the United States is how many American foods were born.[13] All of the barbecue stews have common roots that go back to ancient European, African and Native American stews of grains, beans, squash, fish and meats.[14] Not purely European, African or Native American, the cleverly combined recipes and cooking techniques gave us our traditional American barbecue stews.[15]

Soups and stews are nutritious and economical. This makes them perfect for providing a delicious and nourishing meal for a large group of people at a low cost. During the Great Depression, the U.S. government urged the creation of soup kitchens. Congress enacted legislation to establish the Works Progress Administration (WPA) and provided the funds to purchase sausage for soup kitchens. That's why people now call sausage soup "WPA soup."[16]

A Virginia Tradition

Powhatan Indian–style soup pot at the re-created Powhatan Indian village at Jamestown Settlement living-history museum, Williamsburg, Virginia. *Author's collection.*

People in Wisconsin and the upper Midwest region of the United States have a tradition of making an outdoor stew called "booyah." The stew's origins date back to when Belgian immigrants brought a traditional festival with them known as the Kermiss. In 1858, people in northeast Wisconsin held the first Kermiss in the United States. Celebration, thanksgiving, dancing and feasting were the main themes. The bill of fare included pies, bread and other delicacies, along with huge kettles of booyah cooked in the open air. Today, cooks use meats such as chicken, beef, pork or turtle meat. However, wild game was originally the preferred protein.[17] A booyah recipe that has been around for almost 150 years calls for several quarts of navy beans, twelve stewing chickens, beef, pork and quarts and quarts of other

Brunswick Stew

Stew master Sam Harrison stirring Brunswick stew at the Barbeque Exchange in Gordonsville, Virginia. *Courtesy Craig Hartman.*

good things like cabbage, peas, carrots, tomatoes and rice. The seasoning is just salt and black pepper.[18]

The most accepted account of the origin of the name "booyah" tells us that long ago, a newspaper reporter in Wisconsin asked the local cook what he was going to prepare for a benefit picnic. The response was "bouillon." However, due to the cook's heavy accent, it came out sounding to the reporter like "booyah."[19] Therefore, that is what he wrote down and printed.[20] There was also a Native American stew known as booyah, although no connection between it and the Wisconsin booyah has been identified.[21]

Dundas sheep stew is a traditional Virginia stew from the region in and around the eastern portion of Lunenburg County, Virginia. For as long as anyone can remember, the men of the community have been cooking the sheep stew in large kettles that they stir with long paddles. In addition to the sheep meat, it contains other good things such as potatoes, onions, fatback, salt, red pepper and black pepper and breadcrumbs for thickening. This sheep stew appears to be Lunenburg's version of Brunswick stew. Moreover, like Brunswick stew, Dundas sheep stew is a favorite food served at fundraisers.[22]

Barbecue Hash, Brunswick Stew and Burgoo

Barbecue hash is a simple meat stew that requires long cook times and frequent stirring. In the Charleston area of South Carolina, people eat it over rice. In other regions, people eat it by itself or over grits or bread. Others use it as a sauce for barbecued meats. Recipes vary, with the most basic being just meat and onions. Other recipes call for a variety of additional vegetables, including tomatoes, bell peppers, carrots and potatoes. However, because hash simmers for so long, you can't tell for sure if vegetables are in it or not. Meats used to make barbecue hash include beef, pork, poultry and offal. Offal is the internal organs of animals such as the liver, the kidneys, the heart, the tongue, sweetbreads, the "lights" (lungs) and the "goozle" (windpipe and part of the throat). Barbecue hash can include one or a combination of those depending on the regional variation of the stew being prepared. Consequently, no one should judge barbecue hash by its appearance. Because of the long cook time and constant stirring, it doesn't always look appetizing. However, when properly prepared, it's delicious.

The Brunswick County/Lake Gaston Tourism Association sponsors Brunswick Stew Day every January in Richmond, Virginia. *Author's collection.*

Brunswick stew recipes include various meats such as poultry, beef, pork or wild game or a combination of any of them. The vast majority of recipes always call for tomatoes, potatoes, beans and corn. However, Virginia Brunswick stew originalists make it with only middling, squirrel, onions and breadcrumbs (for thickening).

Burgoo is similar to Brunswick stew, but recipes for it are far more variable. Unlike Brunswick stew, burgoo can be made without a strictly followed recipe. Burgoo recipes can contain just about any vegetable available to the cook, and mutton might be the meat of choice.

The basic seasonings used in all the barbecue stews are salt, black pepper and red pepper. After that, things are open to slight interpretation. Some barbecue stew cooks like to improvise and add their own secret herbs and spices. Although not common, some add bourbon, wine or, in the case of burgoo, bitters to their recipe. Some burgoo cooks season their stew with sassafras or curry powder. There are South Carolinian barbecue hash cooks who add barbecue sauce to their hash, just as some Georgian Brunswick

> To the Editor of the *Dispatch*:
>
> I now desire to give briefly my views with regard to the proper mode of making a Brunswick stew. To make it of the best quality either squirrels or chickens might be used as a basis. But, as the former are rarely obtainable in cities chickens will serve almost as good a purpose. They ought to be boiled very thoroughly and until the meat can be easily separated from the bone. Then add young fresh corn, tomatoes, and butter-beans, and boil until they are done. Season with a sufficient quantity of salt and cayenne pepper. The stew ought to have a liberal quantity of meat and be boiled down to a thick consistency, or until but little liquid is left in it. Brunswick stews in cities are generally made with veal, lamb, or beef as a basis, but all of them are generally inferior to a stew made with chickens. A large majority of these stews have an insufficiency of meat, and are really nothing more nor less than thick soups. Canned corn should never be used. It is generally old, indigestible, and imparts an unpleasant flavor to the stew. A stew such as our country cousins make is indeed a dish good enough for a prince. One made according to the usual city formula is an unmitigated fraud and humbug. Signed, M.D.
>
> *Richmond Dispatch*, "Brunswick Stew. To Know How to Make It a Matter of No Small Importance," June 14, 1891

stew cooks add barbecue sauce to their stew. Virginians save the barbecue sauce for barbecue and bitters for old fashioneds.

All three of the barbecue stews require the same cooking technique. Traditionally, stew masters cook them outside over open fires in iron kettles. First, the meats are simmered until they are pull-tender. At that point, the cook removes the bones and pulls the meat into shreds. Additionally, some cooks chop or grind the meat before returning it to the pot. After the meat is tender and has been pulled and/or chopped, the vegetables go into the pot with the meat according to their required cook time. Most importantly, constant stirring is required, making a long-handled paddle the barbecue stew master's constant companion.

The stew stories, or folklore, involving the barbecue stews includes entertaining songs, stories and poems about the stews and their origins.

COMMONWEALTH OF VIRGINIA
GENERAL ASSEMBLY
HOUSE JOINT RESOLUTION NO. 2 PASSED IN 2002

WHEREAS, by act of the 1988 General Assembly, Brunswick County was proclaimed the birthplace of the "gastronomic miracle" known as Brunswick Stew; and

WHEREAS, despite the attempts of pretenders from other states, Virginia's claim as the capitol of Brunswick Stew was reaffirmed in 1999 when Brunswick County stewmaster Jeff Daniel was declared World Champion of Brunswick Stew; and

WHEREAS, Brunswick Stew has a long and glorious history in the Commonwealth, beginning in 1828, when camp cook Jimmy Matthews, faced with the problem of feeding a hunting party on the Nottoway River, first combined squirrel, bacon, onions, butter, and stale bread into a thick concoction that pleased the members of the party; and

WHEREAS, with the help of former members of the General Assembly Creed Haskins and George Dromgoole, Brunswick Stew later became a fixture at Southside political gatherings; and

WHEREAS, over the years, Brunswick Stew, with the addition of such ingredients as chicken, corn, tomatoes, and lima beans, has become even more ambrosial; and

WHEREAS, when the Brunswick County Chamber of Commerce began a campaign in the late 1980s to promote economic growth in the County, Brunswick Stew served to remind the public of the economic development opportunities in Brunswick County; and

WHEREAS, "Brunswick Stew Day" has since become an honored and popular annual tradition at the Capitol, where hundreds warm their stomachs and spirits with a hearty serving of the "celestial sustenance known as Brunswick Stew"; now, therefore, be it

RESOLVED by the House of Delegates, the Senate concurring, That the fourth Wednesday in January, in 2002 and in each succeeding year, be designated Brunswick Stew Day at the General Assembly; and be it

RESOLVED FURTHER, That the Clerks of the House of Delegates and the Senate be directed to note this auspicious occasion on the official Calendars of the House of Delegates and the Senate so that members may be reminded to partake of the unique delights of the authentic Brunswick Stew.

Barbecue stew folklore was created by people in times past who struggled with issues ranging from slavery to feuds, expanding borders, colonization, civil war, homesickness and isolation in urban and frontier regions. Today, stew stories continue to be important to the people who cherish the stews. Often, the actual history of the stews takes a backseat to the sensational stew stories that have been passed down from generation to generation. Even though barbecue stew folklore is ahistorical and contains everything from half-truths to outright fiction, it is a legacy that reflects a distinctly American history and the unique intercultural exchanges that have occurred throughout the history of the United States.

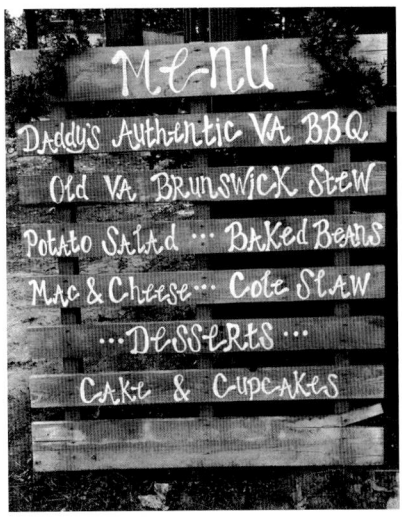

The bill of fare served at a wedding celebration in Virginia demonstrates that Virginians still cherish their barbecue and Brunswick stew. *Author's collection.*

Andrew Zimmern astutley observed, "Food with a story tastes better. Food with a story you haven't heard before tastes better than that."[23] This observation is doubly true regarding the barbecue stews that owe much of their status and appeal to the entertaining stew stories surrounding them. Moreover, everyone knows that food tastes better when dining with good company. The large iron kettles of barbecue stew that can feed hundreds of people bear testimony to the fact that the barbecue stews are meant to be shared. Therefore, be ready to share your favorite stew stories while enjoying a dish of your favorite barbecue stew with friends and family.

Chapter 2
VIRGINIA'S FOOD TRADITIONS

There was hardly a neighborhood in which there was not some favorite spring devoted to barbecuing purposes. The barbecue season generally commenced in May, before which time fish fries and squirrel stews were the order of the day. In every neighborhood there was some person noted as a skillful barbecue cook. The squirrel stew, when well concocted, formed a delicious repast. All sorts of savory condiments were thrown into the cauldron, and its steam was sufficient to make the mouth of an epicure fairly water.
The barbecue proper consisted of shotes and lambs, dressed with a super abundant supply of pepper, and cooked over a large fire built up in holes five or six feet long and three or four deep. Sticks were placed over these, and the shote or lamb laid on it. Vegetables in abundance were always to be had, and the foot of the table was usually graced by a ham of bacon. The table was a temporary affair, made of rough planks, laid upon scantling, and the seats were of the same character. The plates, knives, forks, dishes, pots, etc., were of course contributed by the givers of the feast, and in the evening an ox cart or two generally drove up to take all the materials home. The drink was almost entirely mint juleps, that delicious beverage which is now never had as it used to be in the days of yore.
The principal amusements were ninepence loo, quarter whist, and conversational upon all manner of subjects. It was very rare to see anybody intoxicated, and if one became so, and made himself disagreeable, he was not invited again. Neighborhoods took it by turns to give barbecues. This neighborhood would begin this Saturday, and invite the adjoining neighborhood. That neighborhood would reply next Saturday and then a third, a fourth, and so on.

A Virginia Tradition

Thus nearly every Saturday would witness a barbecue somewhere in the county, and it was kept up until frost came.
—New York Herald, *"The Old Fashioned Barbecue in Virginia,"* April 29, 1858

Virginians have observed their traditional barbecue season for almost four hundred years. No other state in the Union has an older, uninterrupted barbecue tradition. Before the twentieth century, families in Virginia took turns hosting community gatherings of some sort all year long. When the weather turned cold from November to January, Virginians slaughtered hogs in order to smoke the meat for Virginia hams and bacon. Hog killing time was also a time for festivals, as farmers would take turns holding hog killing parties. Virginians used to have a saying, "We had a hog killin'est time," that reflects the lively events.[1] After hog killing season, the months of March and April brought with them the season for fish feasts, "soups" and "stews."

Catching fish from local waters, Virginians served them fried along with ham, fish stews, crabs, clams and oysters from local waters, as well as other delicious foods. Throughout spring and summer, squirrel soup and Brunswick stew were

Delicious Brunswick stew served at Shaffer's BBQ & Market in Middletown, Virginia. *Author's collection.*

cooked outside in large iron pots. Springtime was the planting season, and holding squirrel soup and stew feasts at that time of the year was a way for farmers to protect newly sown crops from pillaging squirrels. Brunswick stew events started before Barbecue Season started in May and continued until the Barbecue Season ended after the first frost arrived in October. Virginia's barbecue season provided a way for communities to gather for fellowship and community feasts in times before refrigeration when it was difficult to store fresh meats in the hot summertime. During the Barbecue Season, Virginia's communities took turns barbecuing whole animal carcasses and invited all to the events. Unlike other states, whose backyard barbecue season tradition started in the twentieth century, Virginia's barbecue season is the original and oldest in the Union and is rooted in Virginia's agrarian past.

Virginia-Style Barbecue

The first English colonists who arrived in Virginia in 1607 brought hogs with them, along with their way of salting pork to preserve it. Shortly after colonists arrived, the Powhatan Indians taught them how to smoke and barbecue the pork the way they smoked and barbecued wild game. Dr. L. Daniel Mouer, who was head of archaeology at Virginia Commonwealth University and co-founder and vice-president of the Culinary Historians of Virginia before retiring, observed, "[U]sing the Indian method of cooking bear or venison, barbecued pork became typical of Virginia's cuisine."[2] This is how what we call southern barbecue was born in Virginia.[3] It is important to keep in mind that the barbecue cooking technique is ancient. However, the origins of the various modern incarnations of it can be identified. For example, the southern version of barbecue, what we call "southern barbecue," has its beginnings in seventeenth-century Virginia.

The English word *barbecue* came from the word *barbacoa*, which is what Spanish conquistadors heard Native Americans in Haiti calling their wooden hurdles and grills. However, the same scholars who discovered that fact are the very ones who also told us that the English word *barbecue* is a "Virginian word" recognizing that Virginia is the birthplace of southern barbecue.[4] In recognition of the collaboration between Virginia's Indians and colonists that created southern barbecue, the 1887 edition of *A New English Dictionary on Historical Principles* (the original edition of the *Oxford English Dictionary*) stated, "The Virginia barbacue [*sic*] and the French boucan were all derived from the names of the high wooden gridiron or scaffolding on which Indians dried, smoked, or broiled their meats."[5]

The fact that the most esteemed scholars of their day identified Virginia with the word *barbecue* is significant for our understanding of barbecue history. The modern and often repeated myth that "barbecue" was born in Haiti and "made its way" to North America from there sometime in the seventeenth century is not supported by the historical record. Native Americans were using wooden barbecue grills all over the Americas before European contact, not just in Haiti. There is no barbecue "line of succession" from Haiti to North America. Native people were cooking their version of barbecue in what is today Virginia at least 10,000 years before natives from South America first reached Haiti's shores 2,500 years ago.[6]

After Europeans arrived in the New World and mingled with Native Americans, various styles of barbecue emerged in several regions of the Americas without influence from one another. Southern barbecue developed in Virginia from Powhatan Indian, African and European cookery without the aid of the faraway and hostile Spanish conquistadors or the Taino Indians in Haiti. The southern style of barbecue reflects the barbecuing technique practiced by the native peoples of Virginia with seasonings introduced by English colonists and people of African descent. Barbecue in the Caribbean, such as Jamaican jerk, has its own independent path of development. The barbecue cooked by Spanish colonists and Mexicans in North America was cooked by burying meat with hot rocks underground, and this style of barbecue is called "barbacoa" to this day. Barbacoa was preserved in the Southwest and in California, where it was advertised to eastern visitors at the turn of the twentieth century as barbecue "à la Mexicana."[7] The common thread in all of those styles of barbecue is the cookery of local Native Americans, not the Taino people of sixteenth-century Haiti. Unfortunately, the origin of the word *barbacoa* in Haiti that became the English word *barbecue* has caused some to confuse the origin of the word *barbecue* with the origin of the barbecue cooking technique. However, it is the word *barbecue* that "made its way" from the Caribbean to Virginia in the seventeenth century and then to the rest of North America, not the barbecue grill or the basic barbecue cooking technique.

Today, Virginia has a thriving barbecue tradition, even if you haven't heard of it on TV or seen it in magazines. Indeed, reports of the death of Virginia-style barbecue are greatly exaggerated. Over the last decade, Virginians have embraced Virginia's own delicious barbecue recipes more strongly than ever. This has resulted in a dynamic renaissance of the Old Dominion's delicious barbecue styles.

In colonial and Federal times, when Virginians departed in order to settle lands to the south and west, they took their barbecue with them. Virginians even treated Texans to their delicious style of barbecue. Early Scott was an African American who was born in Virginia in 1852. By 1869, he had made his way to San Antonio, Texas, and married a woman named Eliza. He and Eliza had three children. By the 1870s, Scott was the operator of a saloon in San Antonio called the Old Gray Mule that featured gambling and a bar on the first floor and dancing on the second. That saloon was famous, or infamous, even into the early twentieth century. By 1910, Scott and his family had moved to El Paso, where he made his living as a cook and "saloonman." Early Scott's menu included typical Texas specialties such as hot tamales, chili con carne and enchiladas. However, at the top of his menu, listed in capital letters, was "OLD VIRGINIA BARBECUE."[8]

In the early seventeenth century, many Virginians tried to emulate the lifestyle of the English nobility. In England, kings and nobles enjoyed grand feasts, and only they could legally hunt deer. In colonial Virginia, anyone could hunt deer and eat venison. Consequently, early colonists and Powhatan Indians invited one another to their outdoor celebrations and festivals. As is often the case in such situations, both groups created a sort of colonial-era fusion cuisine. Colonists introduced Powhatan Indians to foods and seasonings such as salted pork, milk and wheat. The Powhatan Indians introduced the English to cornbread, smoked meat and their style of barbecuing meats. Instead of old England's "ox roasted whole" or carbonadoed venison, such as the king would serve, Virginians enjoyed wild game, beef and hogs barbecued by Powhatan Indians but seasoned with English ingredients such as salt, butter, red pepper, mustard and vinegar. They played the same games that the king of England played, such as cockfighting, horse racing and gander pulling. Gander pulling was a cruel game where men competed to pull the head off a greased goose hung upside down from a tree limb. By the 1640s, those Virginia-style barbecues had become especially popular at weddings and funerals.

In the eighteenth century, Virginians were the first to establish barbecue clubs, and the custom persisted into the late nineteenth century. American poet and author Laughton Osborn (1808–1878) paid homage to Virginia's barbecue clubs in his 1869 drama *The Magnetiser: The Prodigal Comedies in Prose*. In it, a character was asked how he found "the folk in the Old Dominion" during his recent trip to Virginia. He responded, "Such a round

> **Barbecued Meats.**
>
> **OLD VIRGINIA BARBECUE.**
> **HOT TAMALES, CHILE CON CARNE AND ENCHILADAS.**
> Give us 6 hours notice on special orders.
> **E, Scott.**
> Phone 4854.   401 E. Second St.

Early Scott's menu of delicious foods offered to patrons in El Paso, Texas, included "Old Virginia Barbecue." From the *El Paso Herald*, July 18, 1914. *Courtesy Library of Congress.*

of feasting! And that infernal Barbecue-Club! I have nearly drunk my liver into a hepati'is."[9] Although a work of fiction, the dialogue demonstrates that Virginia was famous for its barbecue clubs and club members had a reputation for holding lively meetings.

The Buchanan Spring Barbecue Club, which met near Richmond, Virginia, was one of the most famous. It started in the mid-1700s and continued until the start of the Civil War. Chief Justice John Marshall was a founding member. George Washington, James Madison and Thomas Jefferson attended club meetings from time to time. Club members and their guests met every Saturday or so to enjoy an "old fashioned barbecue under the trees."[10] R.T.W. Duke Sr. and his friends established the Cool Spring Barbecue Club near Charlottesville, Virginia, after the end of the Civil War. R.T.W. Duke Jr. recorded how Juba Garth and his wife, Mandy, who were enslaved until the end of the Civil War, prepared Virginia-style barbecue for the club:

> *The process was as follows: A pit about ten feet long—five feet wide and about 3 feet deep, was dug in the ground & filled with kindling & green wood & set on fire about 5 o'clock in the morning & allowed to burn until it became a mass of glowing red hot coals. In the mean time pigs—quite young ones—& lambs—had been prepared & tied with green withes to two green poles about 6 or 7 feet longer than the pit was wide. They were then stretched over the coals & basted with melted butter in which some boiling water—salt & pepper were mixed. Two men were assigned to each animal, one on each side of the pit & turned the carcass over & over whilst a "baster" basted it with the melted butter.*[11]

Brunswick Stew

In 1875, the "Father of American Fly Fishing," Thaddeus Norris, wrote about three types of Virginia barbecues that existed before the start of the Civil War.[12] One was what he called "the little squirrel barbecue." This was a summertime barbecue held by a small company of friends after a morning of hunting. Hunting commenced at daybreak and continued until about ten o'clock in the morning. At that time, the small band of hunters would head to an appointed place near a cool stream or spring. They used the spring to chill foods and drinks. They constructed a wooden hurdle using sticks just as the Powhatan Indians first taught Virginians to construct in the early seventeenth century. A barbecue hurdle is what we would call today a wooden barbecue grill that rests on four forked posts. They started a fire using hardwood and let it burn down to glowing coals. The young squirrels were cleaned, dressed, seasoned and set on the barbecue hurdle over the coals. They barbecued the young squirrels slowly until they were tender and juicy. The hunters took the "old squirrels" home and used them to make Virginia-style squirrel soup.

Another type of Virginia barbecue mentioned by Norris is the community barbecue. This type of barbecue was often accompanied by a fish fry. Many people from all around the community attended these barbecues, and

Tender, mouthwatering Virginia pork barbecue slathered with Virginia's Southside-style barbecue sauce. *Author's collection.*

everyone who could afford to do so contributed labor, equipment and foods for the events. Large barbecue pits were dug over which a wooden hurdle was placed. Muttons, shoats (young pigs), squirrels and other meats were barbecued. Expert cooks prepared squirrel soup in large kettles seasoned with "onions and smoked middling," which is the original Virginia-style Brunswick stew recipe. The events were very festive, with good food, fellowship and games such as card playing and horse racing.

The third type of Virginia barbecue mentioned by Norris is what he called the "Ladies Barbecue," or the "Dancing Barbecue," where "matrons and maidens who danced were invited to attend." R.T.W. Duke Jr. also mentioned a "ladies' barbecue" in his *Recollections*.[13] This type of barbecue was more formal than the other two types. Attendees arrived in carriages and on horseback wearing their finest apparel. Ribbons adorned the servants and music filled the air, prompting attendees to participate in "reels, cotillions, and jigs." Sometime in the 1840s, the squirrel soup that Norris wrote about became widely known in Virginia as Brunswick stew. This kind of Virginia barbecue was a frequent occurrence "in the days of plenty 'befo' de wah.'"[14] However, according to Norris, by 1875, the frequency at which Virginians hosted this type of barbecue had diminished.

Unlike some North Carolinians, Virginians have rarely used undiluted vinegar mixed with salt and pepper on barbecued meats. Virginians have always added something to the vinegar such as water, butter, lard, mustard and/or tomato to reduce its acidity. By the Virginian standard, eastern North Carolina barbecue sauce is too vinegary, and central Texas and Kansas City barbecue sauce isn't vinegary enough. As Goldilocks would say, Virginia's barbecue sauces are "just right." Tomato in some form has been an ingredient in some Virginia-style barbecue recipes since at least the 1870s and was probably included in earlier times.[15]

As more people prospered and as immigrants brought new foods into the United States, the ingredients used to season barbecue changed with the times in Virginia just as they did everywhere else. Over a period of several years, Mrs. Gibson Jefferson McConnaughey researched, transcribed and experimented with old family recipes handed down from mother to daughter through six generations that lived at Haw Branch Plantation in Amelia, Virginia, built by her ancestors in 1745. McConnaughey's study of the plantation records uncovered several Virginia-style barbecue recipes—one she calls "the old way" and another she calls "the new way." The "old way" calls for a classic colonial and antebellum Virginia-style sauce made with butter, vinegar, salt, black pepper and red pepper. The "new way" recipe reflects how Virginia-style barbecue had changed by the late nineteenth century and early twentieth century. The "new way" recipe adds tomato ketchup, brown sugar and Worcestershire sauce to the "old way" recipe.[16] Today, there are four main styles of Virginia barbecue sauces. There are the tangy sauces of Southside Virginia, which include a hint of mustard; the vinegar-based sauces seasoned with herbs of the Shenandoah Valley; the central Virginia sauces that are perfumed with spices (some there add a little Virginia peanut butter, too); and the sweeter, richer barbecue sauces of Northern Virginia.

Virginia Smoked Ham

Planter William Bullock (1612–1650) recorded in 1649 that there was "an infinite number of Hogges" in Virginia.[17] Eighteenth-century historian Robert Beverly wrote of Virginia in 1705, "Hogs swarm like vermin upon the earth."[18] Union soldiers encountered so many hogs in Virginia during the Civil War that they called them "Virginia rabbits."[19] Some cities had to pass strict ordinances to deal with the free-roaming hogs that filled their streets. Falmouth, Virginia, was nicknamed "Hogtown." These facts bear witness to Virginian's long-held love for and expertise at barbecuing and smoking pork. Since colonial times, Virginia smoked ham has been a delicacy famous the world over. Author and scholar Marshall Fishwick eloquently expressed his admiration for Virginia ham when he wrote, "No self-respecting Southern pig can imagine a higher distinction than becoming, in due course, a Virginia ham—spicy as a woman's tongue, sweet as her kiss, as tender as her love."[20]

As far back as the 1630s, Virginians were exporting their smoked pork to happy customers in England.[21] By 1649, the sale of Virginia smoked pork could enable a man to earn enough money to "woo a good man's daughter."[22] In a 1688 letter to the Royal Society of London, clergyman John Clayton wrote, "[S]wine, they have now in great abundance." He went on to describe Virginia's smoked pork, which was "as good as any Westphalia [considered the finest hams in Europe at the time], certainly far exceeding our English."[23] Hugh Jones, an English clergyman who lived in Virginia for two years, wrote in 1724, "[T]heir [Virginian's] Pork is famous, whole Virginia Shoots [shoats, or young pigs] being frequently barbacued [*sic*] in England; their Bacon is excellent, the Hams being scarce to be distinguished from those of Westphalia."[24] This statement not only illustrates the fame of Virginia's smoked hams but also implies that by 1724, Virginia had become famous for its barbecue and people in England wanted to try their hand at cooking Virginia-style barbecued pork.

An 1841 Pennsylvania newspaper reporter wrote of how diners "smack their lips as heartily as I do over a good old Virginia ham that fairly melts in your mouth."[25] The *Daily Dispatch* reported in 1858, "A delicious Virginia ham on its bed of greens, engirdled by its rim of eggs (a la Old Dominion), and a slice of chicken or turkey, might do very well for a plain country gentleman's dinner for two or three times a week, and these could be had for the asking on every Virginia farm."[26] The nineteenth-century American humorist George W. Bagby wrote in his famous 1877 essay *The Old Virginia Gentleman*, "[A] Virginian could not be a Virginian without bacon and greens. He must have fried chicken, stewed chicken, broiled chicken, and chicken pie; old hare, butter-beans, new potatoes, squirrel, cymlings, snaps, barbecued shoat, roas'n ears, buttermilk, hoe-cake." Bagby continued, "He next gets religion at a camp-meeting, and loses it at a barbecue or fish-fry."

Nicholas Cresswell (1751–1804) recorded an eyewitness account of how colonial Virginians preserved pork. Born in Derbyshire, England, he came to America seeking a better life than he could forge in Europe. However, personal difficulties and the American Revolution compelled him to return to England. He wrote about his time in America between the years 1774 and 1777 in his personal journal. While in Virginia on Tuesday, July 26, 1774, he recorded the following:

> *The bacon cured here is not to be equaled in any part of the world, their hams in particular. They first rub them over with brown sugar and let them lie all night. This extracts the watery particles. They let them lie in salt for 10 days or a fortnight. Some rub them with hickory ashes instead of saltpeter, it makes them red as saltpeter and gives them a pleasant taste. Then they are hung up in the smoke-house and a slow smoky fire kept under them for three or four weeks, nothing but hickory wood is burnt in these smoke-houses. This gives them an agreeable flavor, far preferable to the Westphalia hams, not only that, but it prevents them from going rancid and will preserve them for several years by giving them a fresh smoking now and then.*

The first English colonists in Virginia preserved pork with salt or vinegar. However, they quickly learned that salted pork didn't hold up

Brunswick Stew

A Fish Fry in the Old Dominion

On the Rappahannock River, in the county of Richmond, is the Cobham Park Estate, and on it is to be found one of the most delightful spots for out of doors festive occasions. A large and natural arbor is formed by a noble grape vine which overspreads some trees at the foot of a high bank on the river shore. A spring of pure water is nearby, and a mint bed, fresh and verdant, is immediately contiguous.

Some three or four gentlemen, it may be, would be spending the evening sociably with one of the hospitable entertainers of the neighborhood, when among other matters talked of, a Fish Fry would be proposed, and no sooner mentioned than settled that one should take place, and a day named for the gathering. The gentlemen present were to inform some eight or ten of the neighbors, who were to furnish everything necessary for such an occasion; and each one had the privilege of inviting as many gentlemen as he pleased—so that it was no uncommon thing to see from forty to fifty persons at these social reunions.

One gentleman would furnish fine old ham, cured in a manner peculiar to this section, and juicy and delicious beyond comparison. Another would prepare a shoat. Another a quarter of a lamb. And so on, till the bill of fare would be made complete, including some choice old liquors wherewith to brew the julep, which always flows freely on such occasions. To the gentleman on whose estate the Fry takes place is usually accorded the honor of furnishing the fish, oysters, and crabs, which are invariably caught the morning of the Fry, and of course are perfectly fresh.

The eventful day at length arrives. The spot described is the one selected, and at a very early hour active preparations have commenced. A long table of rough planks is soon erected, with benches of the same material, directly under the arbor, which nature has made so complete as almost entirely to exclude the sun. A number of servants are on the ground, and are busily engaged in cleaning the fish, opening the oysters and preparing the crabs, which are all cooked on the spot, ample arrangements being made for that purpose.

Alexandria Gazette, "A Fish Fry in the Old Dominion," December 1, 1851

well in Virginia's hot summers. Looking to the local Powhatan Indians for inspiration, they started smoking their salted pork just as the Powhatan Indians had been smoking wild game and fish for centuries. The English salt along with the Powhatan-inspired hickory smoke turned out to be the perfect mix. In 1879, a newspaper columnist observed of Virginia's pork smoking process: "There appears to be no limit to the time for which bacon thus treated will keep. The writer has eaten hams over twenty years old which were still fresh and sweet. Indeed an orthodox Virginia housewife does not consider a ham cured until it is at least two years old."[27]

In 1902, the pork industry pioneer P.D. Gwaltney Jr. discovered a smoked ham that had been hanging in one of his company's smokehouses in Smithfield, Virginia, for twenty years. Gwaltney fashioned a brass collar for the ham and jokingly called it his pet. He took it to expositions to demonstrate the preservative powers of Virginia's pork smoking method. *Ripley's Believe It or Not!* featured the ham in 1929, 1932 and 2003. Today, the ham resides in the Isle of Wight County Museum, and it is presumably still edible.

Virginia Fish Feasts

Virginians have held outdoor fish feasts (aka "fish frys") for centuries. In fact, the fish fry is an invention of the Old Dominion. An 1851 edition of the *Alexandria Gazette* recorded, "[A]mong their chief pleasures in the summer season is the Fish Fry—an entertainment known by this title from time immemorial to all lower Virginia."[28] The first Virginian "fish fry" took place on a spring day in 1608. John Smith and his men were traveling on a barge when they encountered an "abundance of fish lying so thicke with their heads above water." Lacking nets, Smith's men attempted to catch the fish with frying pans. That experiment failed, and Smith noted that a frying pan "is a bad instrument to catch fish with." After trial and error, they finally found an effective way to catch the fish: they used their swords to spear them. Smith wrote, "[W]e took more [fish] in one hour than we could all eat." Although frying pans were a bad instrument to catch fish, they turned out to be perfect for cooking them, and the Virginia fish fry was born.[29]

Philip Vickers Fithian was born in New Jersey in 1747. He lived in Virginia between 1773 and 1774 after he became a tutor for the family of Robert Carter at his plantation in Virginia's Northern Neck. Fithian kept a journal of his stay and often mentioned fish feasts and barbecues. He wasn't fond

An advertisement for a gander pull, fish dinner and barbecue at Petersburg, Virginia, circa 1828. *Courtesy Albert and Shirley Small Special Collections Library, University of Virginia.*

of Virginia barbecues or fish feasts and often declined invitations to attend them. Fithian wrote of his response to one invitation, "I declined going and pleaded in ex[c]use unusual & unexpected Business for the School." On another occasion, he wrote, "Ben Mr Taylor, Mr Grubb, & Harry went to the Potowmack to a Fish Feast—Come, Fithian, what do you mean by keeping hived up sweating in your Room—Come out & air yourself—But I choose to stick by the Stuff." The excuse used for declining yet another invitation to a fish feast was "I am uncertain whether my Latinitas will not be a Shackle too heavy to allow me to favour his kind invitation." Rain saved him on one occasion, as he noted, "I had a strong invitation to Dr Thompsons Fish-Feast, but the Rainy Weather hindred [sic]."[30]

In 1824, Henry C. Knight, author of *Letters from the South and West*, described Virginia fish feasts as events that could get rowdy at times. Just as it was with barbecues, Virginians were sure to hold a shooting match before the party was over. Knight wrote, "They sometimes meet, and shoot at a target for a fish-fry. Fish-fries are held about once in a fortnight, during the fish season; when twenty or thirty men collect, to regale on whiskey, and fresh fish, and soft crabs just out of their sloughs, cooked under a spreading tree, near a running stream, by the slaves. Here you may see a forester upsnatch a perch by the gills, and, at one quick drawing through the teeth, strip it clean from the spine; then up with another, and so on to the end."[31] Such behavior could explain Fithian's distaste for the events. However, in 1791, a Frenchman named Ferdinand Bayard traveled through Maryland and Virginia. He described fish feasts as being wholesome events.[32]

VIRGINIA FISH FRY—BILL OF FARE—JULY 4, 1833

Mr. B.—one quarter of a lamb, and drum fish; one gallon of whiskey.
Mr. N.—four bottles of wine; two bottles of old whiskey; oysters, crabs, corn bread, peach.
Mr. W.S.—lard and pig, and brandy.
Mr. B.—a middling of bacon, bread, a quarter of a lamb, two bottles of brandy.
Mr. M.—one gallon of brandy and nutmegs, and what he *pleases*.
Mr. B********—drum fish and crabs.
Mr. G.S.—drum fish.
Dr. B.—loaf bread, loaf sugar.
Dr. S.—spirits and sugar; and professional services, if need be, *gratis*.
Mr. R.W.C.—old ham and suet.
Mr. L.—spirits, one gallon.

American Turf Register and Sporting Magazine (August 1833)

In 1833, the *American Turf Register and Sporting Magazine* published an article about a Fourth of July fish feast held in Warsaw, Virginia, in which the author described them as parties where good food and good friends gathered for good-humored fun. Like barbecues, people attended fish feasts from all walks of life. A nearby spring made the occasions even more festive. Just in case the rowdy behavior got out of hand, medical services were provided free of charge.[33] Fresh fish weren't the only foods served at fish feasts, as a 1905 edition of the *Richmond Times-Dispatch* described. While one group was catching the fish and cleaning them, another group was serving foods such as ham and fried, roasted and barbecued meats.[34] A fish fry could be held near any body of water that could supply fish for the feast. When Spangler Mill in Floyd County, Virginia, was reopened in 1911, a fish fry was held in the Graham Grove near Spangler's Pond. Everyone was invited, and all brought "baskets filled with good things to eat." Spangler's Pond and a nearby river were "seined for fish."[35] An 1851 account of Virginia fish feasts

---

Dreamy and Hazy Indian Summer

These "fish fries" in old Virginia are not to be despised by any means. Young and old can participate and add each his quota to the day's programme. They start early in the morning in wagons, buggies, carriages and on horseback, nobody hurries, the day is before them. They seek a shady grove near the banks of a river or mill-pond. At 12 o'clock preparations begin for dinner. Great hampers of food are opened and the odorous contents are removed to the snowy table cloths spread on the grass, and such contents!—old ham, fried chicken, chicken pie, shoat, lamb pies, cakes, pickles, literally everything, except fish.

The young people who have been fishing in full view, bring in the shinning fish, kicking, fresh from the water. These are speedily prepared and in a few moments the whole community is redolent with the frying fish. The people eat, talk politics, discuss crops, make love and flirt. The little folks romp and roll on the grass—was there ever such a time except at a fish fry?

Richmond Times Dispatch, October 1, 1905

from the *Alexandria Gazette* sheds more light on the events and reflects Fithian's experience of being compelled to attend them:

> [T]*hey* [fish feasts] *were gatherings of very great enjoyment to the neighbors, and to all strangers who were fortunate enough to be in the county at the time; for be assured if one were known to be within anything like a reasonable distance, great pains would be taken to seek him out, and he would be pressingly invited to make one of the party.*[36]

My father has often told me of fish feasts that he attended when he was a youngster growing up in Virginia. A company of friends and family would meet at a large pond or a lake. They used nets to catch the fish. They started a cooking fire and fried the fish in iron skillets. Everyone enjoyed the delicious meal with good company.

Virginia Hoecake

From the earliest colonial days, hoecake made with cornmeal (Indian hoecake) or wheat flour (English hoecake) has been a favorite bread in Virginia. Hoecake was so prevalent in colonial and Federal-era Virginians' diets that in 1793, American poet and diplomat Joel Barlow observed in his poem "The Hasty Pudding" that hoecake is "fair Virginia's pride."

Hoecake recipes in Virginia have changed over the centuries. Some call for hominy, some rice flour, some cornmeal and some a mixture of cornmeal and wheat flour, and others call for just wheat flour. The most basic recipe for hoecake is simply cornmeal and water. Indian women taught colonists in Virginia how to prepare hominy and cornmeal and how to use them to make hoecakes, tamales (called "dainties" by Virginians), corn mush and grits just as they would teach the English settlers in Maryland after that colony was established.[37] British explorer and author Thomas Anburey recorded in his diary in the eighteenth century, "Hoe-cake is Indian corn ground into meal, kneaded into a dough, and baked before a fire, but as the Negroes bake theirs on the hoes that they work with, they have the appellation of hoe-cakes."[38] Although it may be true that some enslaved people may have literally cooked hoecakes on hoes, that practice may not fully explain how the cakes got their name. They could have received their name from the unique device Virginians used for cooking hoecakes.

Old fashioned Virginia-style hoecakes made with wheat flour. *Author's collection*.

Maryland-born Quaker Elizabeth Ellicot Lea wrote of hoecakes in her 1846 cookbook, "These cakes used to be baked in Virginia on a large iron hoe, from whence they derive their name."[39] In 1774, Philip Vickers Fithian, who was no doubt an eyewitness as to how hoecake was cooked, wrote that he "[s]up'd on chocolate, & hoe-Cake, so called because baked on a Hoe before the fire."[40] In 1805, Abraham Edlin shared a recipe for "Indian Hoe Cake" that he ascribed to Captain John Smith in his *A Treatise on the Art of Bread-Making*. The recipe calls for making dough with corn (maize) flour, salt and water and rolling it into thin cakes before baking them on "a hot broad iron hoe."[41]

The "hoe" on which hoecakes were cooked is called a Virginia "bread hoe." In 1888, an author explained that the phrase "John Constant" was slang for cornbread baked "on the bread-hoe."[42] In 1880, merchants were selling new "Gold Coin Cook Stoves" with several accessories, including "2 hoe cake bakers."[43] In 1890, an unusual and undoubtedly ineffective treatment for a toothache was to "slam a hot bread hoe 'ginst his jaw."[44]

The possessions listed in the will of William Mitchell, a Virginian who had moved to Georgia after the Revolutionary War, included two bread hoes that he brought with him from Virginia. Writing about them in 1901, an editor commented, "Many of your readers have heard of the hoe cake, but few of them ever saw a bread hoe on which it was baked."[45] In 1953, the *Daily Times-News* printed an article about a Mrs. William Russell Rogers, who arranged flowers in her home on an "old fashioned oblong corn bread 'hoe.'"[46] Although forgotten by most today, the bread hoe was a fairly well-known device in colonial and Federal Virginia. The earliest mention of the device is from 1771, when John Greenhow's store in Williamsburg, Virginia, advertised "Bread Hoes" for sale.[47] Among the equipment found in her mother's plantation kitchen, Martha McCulloch Williams, the author of *Dishes and Beverages of the Old South*, listed "a biscuit-baker," "waffle-irons" and "a hoe-baker."[48]

The "bread hoe" was a Virginian device. European as well as colonial American bakers used a "baking hoe" to scrape up ashes from their ovens, but this is not the same device as a bread hoe.[49] Another colonial and Federal-era cooking pan that resembles the bread hoe is the "bake-iron." Like the bread hoe, the bake-iron was a flat iron pan. However, unlike the bread hoe, it had an iron handle that allowed it to be suspended on a hook over the cooking fire. While in his nineties, Virginia-born John Jay Janney (1812–1907) recorded everything he could remember about life in early nineteenth-century Virginia. He wrote about Virginia hoecake, "But what some thought was the best was the 'hoecake.' We did not bake it before the fire on a hoe but on the bake iron in a large cake about half or three quarters of an inch thick, and baked on both sides."[50] The "hoe" referred to by Janney was a bread hoe, not a farm tool. In the November 28, 1886 edition of the *Cleveland Leader*, Virginia-born author Marion Harland described Virginia bread hoes as being "round, broad, with a short, stout handle like that of a frying-pan, and had a rim around the edge about an inch in height. Sometimes it had three stubby feet, sometimes none."

Some theorize that the word *hoecake* is derived from the old English word *hough*, which referred to a plot of land shaped like a hill. The shape of the hill reminded people of the shape of the cakes.[51] However, that theory doesn't account for Fithian's eyewitness account of the cakes being cooked on a hoe.

Describing how Canadian Indians prepared corn cakes in the 1530s, the French explorer Jacques Cartier wrote that they pounded the corn into flour using wooden mortars and made it into "small loaves, which they set on a broad hot stone and covered them with hot pebbles."[52] This is similar to how Powhatan Indians cooked cornbread and tuckahoe bread on flat, broad, oblong stones set near burning coals. American historian Edward Eggleston wrote in 1894, "The cake which the Indians baked on a hot stone was cooked in New England on a pewter plate, set half on edge before the fire; but the Southern pioneer's wife baked it on a hoe kept for the purpose, calling it a 'hoe-cake.'"[53]

Mary Randolph (1762–1828) is the author of a cookbook titled *The Virginia Housewife*. She was born in Goochland County, Virginia, and had

Powhatan Indian–style hoecakes at the re-created Powhatan Indian village at Jamestown Settlement living-history museum, Williamsburg, Virginia. *Author's collection.*

family ties to Thomas Jefferson. According to culinary historian Karen Hess, Randolph's cookbook was the most influential cookbook of the nineteenth century. Randolph's recipe for journey cake (a New England version of hoecake) is the only recipe in her cookbook that calls for food to be cooked on a wooden board set aslant before a fire.[54] One can only guess as to why Randolph chose a recipe for New England's journey cake rather than Virginia's hoecake. Anne Howe's 1839 cookbook, *The American Housewife*, contains recipes for both journey cakes and hoecakes. That fact strongly implies that in earlier times, Americans differentiated between the two. At some point, cookbook authors started to regard hoecake and journey cake as different names for the same recipe. A hoecake recipe printed in an 1895 edition of the *New England Kitchen Magazine* instructs us to cook the cakes on a "floured board" that is "slanted before the open fire." If no board is available, the author continues, hoecakes can "be baked on a smooth flat stone." The author pointed out that cooking hoecake on a board or a rock is "the original fashion."[55]

The techniques for cooking hoecake and journey cake were adopted from Native Americans. Powhatan Indians used stone and wooden garden hoes, and those tools may have performed double duty as "bread hoes" in Powhatan kitchens.[56] Multipurpose tools were not unheard of among Native Americans. Archaeologists in Texas discovered stone tools used by Native Americans that served double duty as griddles used for cooking.[57] The Powhatan Indian griddles made of flat stones could very well be the inspiration for the Virginia bread hoe. Although similar, it appears that recipes for New England journey cake and the Virginia hoecake developed independently of each other. In New England, Native Americans and colonists cooked the cakes on planks propped up beside the cooking fire. In Virginia, Native Americans cooked them on flat stones, and colonists cooked them on flat bread hoes that mimicked the Powhatan stone griddles. The interchangeableness of the names probably developed merely from the similarities of the recipes.

Tuckahoe, also known as the "Virginia truffle," is a tuber that Powhatan Indians used to make bread.[58] The American scholar James Hammond Trumbull wrote of *tuckahoe*, "The word is not derived from the Indian word for 'bread' but the word for *loaf* or *cake*…and signifies that which is made round, or rounded."[59]

In colonial times, English colonists learned to mix tuckahoe with corn or rice flour to make little round cakes called "Indian bread."[60] This practice implies that the name for these Indian tuckahoe cakes could have eventually been shortened from "Indian tuckahoe cakes" to "Indian hoecakes" and, finally, "hoecakes." This is supported by the fact that Virginians living in the Tidewater region came to be known as "Tuckahoes" because of their great fondness for hoecakes.[61]

Some have conjectured that the word *hoecake* is a mispronunciation of the word *nocake*. The evidence for that theory comes from the writings of William Wood, who lived in New England from 1629 to 1633, and a Puritan named Roger Williams. In 1635, Wood wrote about an Indian food called "nocake" described as "the best of their victuals for their journey." It was corn that had been "parched in hot ashes" and beaten to powder. They carried it in sacks they wore on their backs. The custom was to eat three "spoonefulls" of it three times a day. In 1643, Williams wrote that "[n]okehick" was "[p]arch'd meal, which is a readie very wholesome food, which they eate with a little water, hot or cold."[62]

Others have conjectured that the name "journey cakes" is a nickname for the eat-on-the-go nocake. "Johnnycakes," some claim, may be a distortion of the name "journey cakes."[63] Alternatively, others claim that "johnnycakes" refers to the New England version of hoecake because the name "Johnny" has long been associated with New England.[64] However, New England's Indians ate nocake as a dry powder washed down with water. There was no "cake" (no pun intended) involved. The eastern Algonquian word *nocake* doesn't mean the same thing as the English phrase "no cake." The similarity of pronunciation is purely coincidental.

In addition to hoecakes, Powhatan Indians cooked what we call today tamales. John Smith described the Powhatan process: "Their corne they rost [roast] in the eare greene, and bruising it in a morter of wood with a Polt, lappe it in rowles [rolls] in the leaves of their corne, and so boyle it for a daintie."[65] Just as these dainties are Virginian tamales, hoecake is Virginia's version of the Mexican tortilla, the Venezuelan arepa and Indian frybread. The recipes and cooking methods for all of those are very similar and exhibit clear Native American origins. In fact, frybread is essentially a hoecake recipe that is fried in grease rather than baked on a griddle. Like tortillas, frybread and arepas, hoecakes are round in shape and may be thick or thin. For example, in 1856, a restaurant in Washington, D.C., advertised "thin hot Corn Hoe Cakes."[66] Powhatan Indians used to make "round balls and cakes" as well as "flatt" cakes using cornmeal or hominy.[67] "Thin" and "flat" are characteristics shared by hoecakes, tortillas, arepas and frybread regardless of whether the cakes are made with corn or wheat or a mixture of the two.

Powhatan Indian–style tamales, called Virginia "dainties," at the re-created Powhatan Indian village at Jamestown Settlement living-history museum, Williamsburg, Virginia. *Author's collection.*

The eighteenth- and early nineteenth-century historian William Dunlap described Virginia as "the land of Hog, homminey [*sic*] & hoe-cake." This description underscores the importance of smoked pork and "Indian corn" in colonial and Federal-era Virginians' diets.[68] In the late 1700s, a poet quipped, "It's bacon, bacon, is their fare; They'd sooner choose to live on air, Than too much fresh, or too much fish, For bacon's the Virginian's dish."[69] The Virginian diet of pork and hominy eventually spread to become important parts of the southern diet as well.[70]

The early Virginia colonists, most of whom were men without training as cooks, did not independently develop the recipe for hoecake using a grain that many of them had never seen or eaten before arriving in Virginia. Moreover, Europeans were not aware of the process required to make hominy by boiling maize in water containing a high alkaline lye produced by wood ash before contact with people of the Americas.[71] This process, called nixtamalization, releases the nutrients in corn, which protects people who eat a mainly corn-based diet from developing a nutritional deficiency called pellagra.[72] Numerous cases of pellagra occurred in Europe that resulted from eating maize without applying the Native American nixtamalization process. Moreover, some historians have postulated that pellagra played a part in creating the conditions that caused Jamestown's Starving Time.[73]

The Powhatan Indians provided their "rockahomin," what we call today hominy and corn, and the English provided the pork. Colonists, Native Americans and enslaved people of African descent in Virginia eventually became dependent on both of those two important foods. As Virginian author Roon Frost wrote, "Fondness for pork was one of the few points of agreement between the Indians and the Virginia settlers."[74]

Chapter 3
SQUIRREL SOUP

[T]*he citizens of Tyler* [in Virginia until 1863] *took a notion to have a squirrel hunt, not so much for the pleasure of the sport itself as for the sake of their corn crops, which were in danger of annihilation from the destructive propensity of this vicious quadruped. Two parties were accordingly assembled, numbering thirty each, and upon a bet of a dinner for the whole company, set out for their respective neighborhoods, to make a trial of their skill in that most delightful of all sports—hunting. At the end of the second day, we believe, they returned to headquarters, to make report of their achievements to their several commanders. After all the scalps had been counted, and fair calculations made, the result proved as follows, viz: For one party six thousand and seventy six! For the other seven thousand and fourteen!! Making in all upwards of thirteen thousand squirrels which had been killed and scalped in* two days *by* sixty men. *Marvel not reader. Strange as the above may seem, it is nevertheless true, as our informant can prove to the satisfaction of all who will take the trouble to pay a visit to Fishing creek, the scene of this prodigious performance, where they shall be permitted to feast their eyes on the skeletons, all that remain since the dinner of the immortal thirteen thousand.*
—Alexandria Gazette, *"Great Squirrel Hunt," August 20, 1837*

A writer for *Harper's New Monthly Magazine* once proclaimed that "every American mouth waters at the mention of savory squirrel stew."[1] That was 1859. Although still popular among some Americans, squirrel meat had a much broader appeal in times past than it does today. The flesh of young squirrels is tender and sweet. Therefore, in Virginia, they were often barbecued or roasted. The flesh of older squirrels is tough, stringy and lean. Therefore, the Virginian strategy for cooking them was to simmer the meat until it was tender. Eventually, squirrel gravy, squirrel soup and squirrel stew became Virginian and, later, American staples.

Bearing witness to the American fondness for eating squirrel meat are the numerous nineteenth-century cookbooks that include at least one recipe for cooking it. Three of the most notable are *The Virginia Housewife*, *Housekeeping in Old Virginia* and *The Kentucky Housewife*. Some of the old squirrel soup recipes are simple, calling for just squirrel and vegetables. Others call for richer ingredients such as egg yolks, cream, wine and spices such as cloves and mace. There is an old saying: "Take the squirrel out of squirrel soup and you have most any kind of soup." The saying reflects the fact that recipes for squirrel soup were often simple and nondescript elevated to a higher level of culinary excellence only by the addition of squirrel meat. Homemaker Fanny Lemira Gillette (1828–1926) included a recipe for squirrel soup in her best-selling *White House Cookbook* (published in 1887), which, ironically, has no recipes that came from the White House in it. Although Gillette's squirrel recipe is for soup, it is very similar to Virginia's classic Brunswick stew recipe calling for squirrel, corn, potatoes, tomatoes and lima beans. Gillette wisely cautions the reader to "strain the soup through a coarse colander when the meat has boiled to shreds, so as to get rid of the squirrel's troublesome little bones."

Although Americans loved squirrel soup, they hated squirrels. As early pioneers settled new frontiers, they established farms and plantations. They cleared large fields for growing crops and raising livestock. The surrounding trees created very favorable conditions for squirrels to thrive and multiply near the large fields full of good things to eat. Seeds sowed by farmers provided an abundant source of food. Consequently, squirrel populations in such areas could soar into the tens of thousands. The swarms of squirrels decimated crops, and farmers spent much energy and money in attempts to rid their fields of them.

As people moved farther south and west in the eighteenth and early nineteenth centuries, the front lines of the war against the insatiable vandals moved with them. A popular strategy to rid farms of squirrels was to organize hunting contests. A company of hunters separated into two teams. Each team set out to kill the most squirrels. The losing team was obligated to pay the expense of giving a hearty meal or a barbecue for the victors.

The community squirrel hunt was another strategy used against the bright-eyed marauders. These squirrel hunts ended with community picnics and barbecues where an honored community cook took charge of cooking the quarry from the day's hunt. The soup master cooked squirrel soup outside in iron kettles, and the entire community enjoyed it among friends and family. It was farmers' efforts to rid their farms of pests coupled with opportunities to throw festive parties with plenty to drink and a large pot of tasty squirrel soup to eat that played a significant role in the development of the American taste for squirrels.

There are three categories of squirrels in the United States: ground squirrels, tree squirrels and flying squirrels. One of the most common squirrel species is the eastern gray squirrel. Gray squirrel litters are usually born between February and March, depending on the weather. In years when food is abundant, many females bear a second litter between the months of May and June. The gestation period is about forty-four days. Litter sizes generally range from one to four kits but can include as many as eight.[2] Given favorable conditions, squirrels can multiply quickly. When conditions are not so favorable, squirrels will migrate in great numbers in search of food.[3] In our times, squirrels are generally only a menace to bird feeders and flower gardens. In times past, they were a serious threat to farmers' livelihoods. Squirrels not only dug up seeds immediately after farmers planted them, but they also destroyed crops while they were growing.

In a 1901 letter to the editor of the *Richmond Dispatch*, the writer stated that there were "thousands of squirrels hereabouts [in Spotsylvania County] for every huntsman." The letter went on to describe how the "robbers" destroyed farmers' crops:

> *Deep down in the woodlands, where the sun only filters through the leafy filigree in spangles of shimmering light, the squirrels are working from early dawn until long past twilight. This is their busiest season. They have a thousand and* [one] *things to do—a thousand joys, and as many sorrows. Eternal vigilance is the price of their safety, for hourly the thunderous report of a shotgun summons one of their numbers from some lofty hickory to death—and ultimate dissolution in Brunswick stew. And yet life is so full of pleasure for them now! Bordering the woodlands are the cornfields. On every skeleton cornstalk there is an ear of corn. Squirrels delight in wreaking vengeance on man by robbing these fields.*[4]

A Virginia Tradition

That report leaves little doubt as to why people in Spotsylvania County, Virginia, regularly held barbecues and fish feasts for several decades around the turn of the twentieth century with a main attraction of the events being squirrel soup or Brunswick stew.[5]

During World War I, ground squirrels in California caused $30 million worth of damage to crops statewide. When adjusted for inflation, that is equivalent to more than $717 million today. In response, authorities organized "squirrel drives" with the motto "Death to the Squirrel." The California solution to the problem in those days was to poison the pests.[6] In colonial and Federal times, farmers and plantation owners all over the South and Midwest fought squirrels by shooting them. Nineteenth-century naturalist John Davidson Godman was traveling through Ohio in 1822 and witnessed the destructive power of squirrels firsthand:

> *Parts of the country appeared to swarm with squirrels, which were so numerous that, in travelling along the high road, they might be seen scampering in every direction; the woods and fields might truly be said, in the country phrase, to be "alive with them." A farmer, who had a large field of Indian corn near the road, informed us, that notwithstanding the continued exertions of himself and his two sons, he feared he should lose the greater part of his crop, in addition to his time and the expense of ammunition used in killing and scaring off the little robbers. This man and his sons frequently took stations in different parts of the field, and killed squirrels until their guns became too dirty longer to be used with safety; yet they always found, on returning, that the squirrels had mustered as strongly as before. During this journey, we frequently met squirrel-shooters heavily laden with this game, which in many instances they had only desisted from slaying from want of ammunition or through mere fatigue.[7]*

John Bradbury was a Scottish botanist who visited the midwestern and western United States in the early nineteenth century. He wrote of how squirrels damaged crops and of how farmers dealt with the threat:

> *The squirrels have greatly increased since the country has become populated by the whites, owing to the greater quantity of food afforded, by the opportunities they have of robbing the corn and wheat fields; but the farmers occasionally give what they call "a barbeque" in the woods, to the young riflemen, on the condition that they make a match at squirrel hunting, of six, eight, or ten, against a similar number, who also make a wager amongst*

themselves. The hog is killed, dressed, and roasted after the Indian method; this consists of digging a hole, the bottom of which they cover with hot stones; on these the hog is laid, and covered also with heated stones. There is plenty of liquor, and the frolick ends in shooting at a mark. I have heard of more than 2,000 squirrels being killed at one of these hunts, all with ball.

Bradbury concluded, "The squirrels are the greatest enemy the farmers have now to contend with, but are prevented from an inordinate increase by the frequency of squirrel hunts by the riflemen, which is encouraged by the landowners."[8]

In 1822, squirrels were overrunning farms in and around Chillicothe, Ohio. The *Alexander Herald* reported, "[I]t is impossible to describe the havoc and destruction made by the gray and black squirrels. Whole fields of corn, from five to ten acres, are wholly destroyed; not an ear left." In an attempt to save the crops from total destruction, hunters there killed almost 20,000 squirrels in a single week.[9] That same year, two hundred hunters near Columbus, Ohio, killed 19,680 squirrels in three days.[10] In 1836, forty hunters banded together in Windsor, Massachusetts, for a "grand squirrel hunt"; those hunters killed 17,357 squirrels.[11]

On at least one occasion, Virginia's farmers called in the army to assist them. In October 1803, Captain Andrew Fulton of the Augusta County militia assembled his company of soldiers to defend the Old Dominion from invading hordes of bushy-tailed plunderers. He divided his men into two hunting parties. In a single day, they produced 8,311 "scalps." The soldiers celebrated with "an elegant dinner."[12] Barbecued squirrel and squirrel soup were no doubt the main courses. On a single day in April 1805, hunters in Madison County, Virginia, produced more than 8,800 squirrel scalps.[13]

In some regions, the government established laws to fight the tree-dwelling acrobats. In 1749, authorities in Pennsylvania offered a bounty of three pence (pennies) for every squirrel killed. In that year alone, they paid out £8,000. One English pound was equal to 240 pennies. That means that in the span of a year, local governments in Pennsylvania paid bounties for 640,000 squirrels, for an amount equivalent to what today is a little over $1.63 million. Obviously, that practice didn't last long, but not because they were running out of squirrels—they were running out of money. After local authorities complained that the bounty payments were depleting their treasuries, they reduced the payment per squirrel to a penny and a half before eventually ending the bounty program altogether.[14] Virginia's government also passed laws meant to combat squirrels. However, Virginians didn't offer

A Virginia Tradition

A Georgia stew master stirring the simmering Brunswick stew, while pit masters turn the barbecuing meats. From *Harper's Weekly*, November 9, 1895. *Author's collection.*

a bounty; they levied a fine. Virginia's House of Burgesses considered laws that required Virginians to kill nettlesome squirrels as long ago as at least 1727.[15] In 1790, Virginia's legislators passed a law that required every able-bodied free man in certain counties to deliver twelve squirrel scalps per year to the local justice of the peace or pay a fine of three pence for each of the twelve squirrel scalps they failed to deliver.[16]

Take Two Squirrels and Call Me in the Morning

Beyond savoring the flavor of squirrel soup, people used to believe that it had medicinal powers. Physicians even prescribed it as a treatment for illness. When his daughter, Mildred, took a squirrel for a pet, Confederate general Robert E. Lee joked that she should make the family a special treat of a Virginian specialty, "squirrel soup thickened with peanuts." When the squirrel bit a guest, Lee joked that the best way to cure the bite was with squirrel soup.[17]

Colonel William H. Crook was a White House employee for fifty years, serving fifteen presidents from Lincoln to Wilson. On July 2, 1881, an assassin fired two bullets into President James A. Garfield's abdomen. Two months later, still suffering from his wounds, Garfield remained in critical condition. The "consulting surgeons" recommended squirrel soup as a treatment.[18] Being deeply concerned about the president's health, Colonel Crook decided to take action. He petitioned authorities for a special permit to hunt squirrels on the grounds surrounding the building housing the president. Even so, according to Crook, he never got word from the doctors to deliver the squirrels. However, in an apparent attempt to reassure the public, about two weeks before President Garfield died on September 19, 1881, many newspapers reported that he "was fed on a rich squirrel soup."[19]

The belief that squirrel soup had healing powers persisted into the twentieth century. In 1958, the director of law enforcement for Kentucky's Fish and Wildlife Resources sought legal advice from Kentucky's attorney general on whether a doctor's prescription of squirrel soup for a sick person is a valid legal defense for hunting squirrels out of season. According to Kentucky's attorney general, such a prescription is no excuse to violate hunting laws.[20]

After claiming that he had received "a definite call from the Lord" in 1937, forty-five-year-old Cumberland mountain trapper Jackson Whitlow

Mrs. Fearnow's Delicious Brunswick stew. *Courtesy Boone Brands.*

went on a fifty-three-day fast. He broke the fast when, according to him, God gave him permission to do so. According to Whitlow, God prescribed squirrel broth as his first post-fast meal.

Newspapers took an interest in Whitlow's penance and widely reported it. However, not everyone was sympathetic with Whitlow's cause. One writer commented that his fast-breaking meal of squirrel soup was "a reversal of the order of feeding nuts to squirrels."[21] At any rate, Whitlow didn't like the squirrel soup and soon revealed that God told him that he could have some broth made with beef heart. That didn't help either, so Whitlow sought medical assistance. His doctor prescribed "a diet of two tablespoons of squirrel broth" along with very small amounts of beef broth, milk and orange juice every two hours.[22]

Virginia "Soups"

When most of western Virginia still comprised the frontier regions, settlers and frontiersmen assembled hunting parties to rid the region of the squirrel menace. Men would get up early in the morning to go squirrel hunting. When they returned home, they found other members of the community busily preparing vegetables, bread, cakes and pies. Cooks put the squirrel meat into pots simmering over open fires to make soup or stew. Sometimes the only ingredients available were the squirrel meat and seasonings such as salt and "home-raised pepper," or what we would call red pepper. On other occasions, the pot contained seasonal vegetables along with the meat. Virginians eventually began calling those festive events "soups."[23] The "Virginia soup" was an event much like a barbecue or a picnic. Invited guests brought either game meats or, if game meats weren't available, dressed poultry. Poultry became a common replacement for squirrel because as an area's population grew and towns and cities were established, there were fewer squirrels available. The host of the soup provided the vegetables and seasonings. The cooks put the vegetables and meats into large iron pots over open fires. They were careful to stir the pots constantly with wooden paddles to prevent the contents from scorching.

Young adults and children attending the soups often volunteered to stir the pots with long-handled paddles, and they made a game of it. They would walk around the bubbling kettles stirring the soup with their homemade paddles while singing a spirited song. When the paddle of a young

Brunswick Stew

woman clicked against a paddle held by a young man—inadvertently or otherwise—he could "claim a penalty," which meant that she was obliged to give him a friendly kiss…if he could catch her. Before long, Virginians, and later West Virginians, called those events "kissing soup parties." As the frolicking would get lively from time to time, an older person was always around to chaperone and rescue the soup from the danger of scorching if the need arose.[24]

During the very early days of the Civil War, Stonewall Jackson stationed a company of men in the area of western Virginia that would become a part of West Virginia in 1863.[25] Seeking to supplement their rations, the soldiers resorted to stealing chickens from locals and used them to make chicken soup. This eventually gave rise to the belief that stolen poultry makes superior soup, Brunswick stew and burgoo. For several years after the end of the Civil War, veterans met at annual reunions to hold "grand soups." In homage to the foraging that they resorted to during the war, they decreed that stolen chickens were required in order to hold a proper soup. However, instead of stealing chickens from strangers for their grand soup events, the veterans agreed that they would only "steal" chickens from one another.[26]

Young people stirring the soup pot. From *Jack of All Trades* by Daniel Carter Beard, 1900. *Author's collection.*

A Virginia Tradition

Before Brunswick stew and burgoo were elevated to their exalted positions at festive gatherings and barbecues, squirrel soup was the dish of honor at such events. In that sense, squirrel soup was as much a barbecue soup as Brunswick stew is a barbecue stew. In fact, two of the barbecue stews, Brunswick stew and burgoo, are modern descendants of the simple squirrel soup of earlier times.[27]

When squirrels invaded Powhatan County, Virginia, in the fall of 1907, hunters killed so many squirrels that people there grew "heartily tired" of eating meal after meal of Brunswick stew.[28] Many Virginians of that era turned up their noses at Brunswick stew made with anything but squirrel meat even if they did get their fill of it during squirrel invasions. A newspaper columnist recorded that sentiment when a senior citizen of Richmond, Virginia, reportedly stated in 1903, "Chicken, Indeed! No, sir-ee! No chicken for me in Brunswick stew. Why, don't you know that nothing but young squirrel gives the gamey flavor that is necessary?"[29] The association that Brunswick stew has always had with squirrel meat is a throwback to Virginia's colonial squirrel soup. Over time, Virginians improved the communal squirrel soup recipe, turning it into a thick squirrel stew that was similar to barbecue hash. Eventually, it evolved into what we know today as Brunswick stew. In 1855, a writer for the *Alexandria Gazette* recorded one of the earliest written accounts, embellished with details, of the origin of Brunswick stew, describing how it evolved from Virginia's squirrel soup:

> *In the merry and good old fashioned days, there prevailed in the good old County of Brunswick, Virginia, a most neighborly and social practice. In the proper season of the year, when summer's vegetable gifts abound, and when summer's heat invites to cool springs and shady bowers, it was the custom of the different neighborhoods to repair almost every Saturday to some spring to spend half the day. For the entertainment inwardly of the company a sufficient number of squirrels were shot, and in the absence of a supply of them, chickens were to do the duty and often they were used in combination. These articles were placed in a pot with a sufficient quantity of water and set to stewing over a slow fire. In due time were added tomatoes, corn, butter-beans, potatoes, with the requisite condiments of salt and Cayenne pepper, all of which, when properly cooked, furnished the participators a feast which Apicius, might have envied. This "Brunswick Stew" was, in every respect but one, equal to Meg Merrilies' famous compound in Guy Mannering, and exception is this: Meg's pottage abounded in greater variety of game, for her larder consisted of the game*

preserves of the nobility. You know now, neighbor, what is the origin of the "Brunswick Stew," and we appeal to the Meades and the Turnbulls hereabouts to say if we have not given it correctly.[30]

The *Indianapolis News* reported in 1905 that Brunswick stew was the "dish of all dishes which was born in Virginia" and "the pride of every first-class Virginia cook."[31] Bearing witness to how Brunswick stew was descended from the old-time Virginia farmer's squirrel soup, American author Marion Harland wrote in 1906 that Brunswick stew started as a "Virginia stew of squirrels" and has since been "eaten in perfection at Old Virginia races, 'barbecues' and political dinners."[32]

Burgoo is also a descendant of Virginia's squirrel soup. As settlers moved into Kentucky, they had the same problems with squirrels there that they left behind in the East. At some point, Kentuckians gave squirrel soup the name "burgoo," and as they moved west out of Kentucky, they took burgoo with them. As one writer observed in 1903, "It seems that 'burgoo' was originally squirrel stew, but it has 'evoluted,' to use an expression of Dr. Chauncey Depew, until it has come to a grand old stew of all sorts of meats and vegetables—old because of the length of time during which it is allowed to simmer over a log fire."[33] After savoring a tin cup full of burgoo cooked by

---

ANTEBELLUM BRUNSWICK STEW IN BUCKINGHAM COUNTY, VIRGINIA

Being tired of the fried chicken and other every day Virginian dishes, the decree went forth for a Brunswick stew. That very evening, the squirrels were fetched from the tops of the tall oaks in the forest hard by, the garden furnished the vegetables, and the next day it was served copiously, superbly, royally, under a grand walnut tree, whose mighty Briarrean [sic] arms shaded half the yard. There was no other dish but the Brunswick stew, and that was enough; for it contained all the meats and juices of the forest and garden magnificently conglomerated and sublimed by the potent essence of fiery Cayenne, pod upon pod, lavishly thrown in. A dish capacious as the Mediterranean held it, and it towered aloft like Vesuvius, smoking gloriously.

Southern Literary Messenger 37, no. 5, "Good Eatings" (May 1863)

Stirring twenty gallons of Brunswick stew for a Patawomeck Indian tribe event in Stafford, Virginia. *Author's collection.*

the burgoo king James Looney, J.A. Estes, the editor of *Blood Horse* magazine, noticed the use of squirrel meat in the burgoo and rhymed, "Two dozen squirrels shed their skin; before the cooking fire begins."[34]

In 1919, author Irvin Bacheller described the way early settlers in Indiana often had to go "round the field and scare the squirrels out." The abundance of squirrels coupled with the desire to eliminate the pests resulted in the farmers frequently holding a "squirrel burgoo." "[E]verybody turned out for a day and shot squirrels," Bacheller wrote. He continued, "We skinned them and stewed them in a sugar kettle with pork and potatoes and onions and perhaps a rabbit or two. Then everybody sat down and enjoyed himself."[35] Samuel Corbaley, a "well known and respected citizen" of Indiana, wrote of the damage done by squirrels to crops there in the 1840s:

> *I was born in Wayne Township* [Indiana] *in 1834, and can remember when, in the early forties, the squirrels (black and gray) were so plentiful they almost destroyed the young corn. I think it was the spring of '43 that my father's neighbors proposed to kill all the squirrels around his farm if he would furnish the bread for a burgoo. A day was appointed, and corn bread enough for a small army baked by my mother and the neighbor women. Three large iron sugar kettles, filled with water, were hung up near a spring. Beverly Ballard, a Kentuckian, was appointed chief cook. The neighbors, with rifles, approached the farm from every direction, and there was a continuous fusillade until 10 o'clock, when, by agreement, the hunters met, and threw down not less than two hundred squirrels. As they were skinned and washed, they were handed over to the cook for boiling. Then followed a feast. Soup was served in tin cups; squirrels were taken out whole with pointed sticks, and corn pone was served with soup made hot with home-raised pepper. After dinner, the targets were set up and there was a test as to the best shot; and many times the center was hit at a distance of twenty, forty and fifty yards.*[36]

This old account makes it clear that the burgoo of that era was often no more than squirrel soup. It wasn't a thick, rich stew as it is today. When ready to eat, the servers used pointed sticks to remove whole squirrel carcasses from the pots and served them in tin cups with the thin, soupy broth.

More than merely hunters' stews, Brunswick stew and burgoo are deeply rooted in both Virginia's and Kentucky's agrarian past. The squirrel meat traditionally used in Brunswick stew and burgoo harkens back to when frontier farmers defended their crops from pillaging squirrels. The vegetables they used in the stews grew from the very plants the farmers were protecting from the voracious rodents. Farmers combined both the vegetables and the squirrel meat to make delicious squirrel soup from which, eventually, both Virginia's Brunswick stew and Kentucky's burgoo would be born.

Chapter 4
BARBECUE HASH

The [barbecued] meats were done to a turn, and the hash—well, the gods of Olympus would have pitched their ambrosia out of their plates, and rushed pell-mell in search of [barbecue] hash.
—News and Herald, "The Old Sixth," August 9, 1879

According to an old saying, "Spoons may not be as old as the world, but they are as old as soup." In seventeenth-century Virginia, forks were rare luxuries enjoyed only by the wealthiest families. Even when a family could afford forks, they owned precious few. When wealthy planter Richard Hobbs of Rappahannock County died in 1677, a single fork was among his most cherished possessions. The scarcity of forks wasn't only a Virginian problem. Hosts in seventeenth-century France often expected invited guests to bring their own forks to dinners and banquets.

Although forks were rare in Virginia's colonial and Federal eras, just about everyone had at least one spoon. Wealthy people had spoons made of tin, pewter and silver. Poor colonists, Native Americans and enslaved people sometimes made spoons out of wood or oyster and mussel shells. The scarcity of forks and the resulting importance of spoons continued as Virginians moved out of the Tidewater region to open new frontiers. As late as the early nineteenth century, Virginians living in rural communities were still using forks only on special occasions. Therefore, it shouldn't be surprising that many of the foods cooked and eaten in colonial and Federal times were spoon-friendly soups, stews and hashes.[1]

Cooking the ingredients in stews into a single "stewy" mass with few discernable ingredients is an ancient practice. American colonists used to call such foods "spoon-meats" because they could be eaten with a spoon.[2] The frequent pot stirring required when making spoon-meat resulted in a soft, filling, easy-to-eat food especially favored by the toothless members of the household. Sometimes the cook chopped the ingredients, which helped them soften more quickly.

According to Samuel Johnson's *A Dictionary of the English Language*, published in 1755, the English verb *hash* means "to mince or chop into small pieces, and mingle." From the verb *hash* came the noun *hash*, which refers to foods that cooks chop or mince and mix. Therefore, in a sense, spoon-meat is a hash. However, there is one aspect of hash that was not necessarily true of spoon-meat. Hash provides a way to disguise leftover or otherwise unappetizing foods. Spoon-meat may have disguised its ingredients simply because they almost melted into the stew; however, unlike hash, it appears that characteristic was more a byproduct than a purpose of the dish.

Barbecue hash and rice at Bessinger's BBQ in Charleston, South Carolina. *Author's collection.*

A Virginia Tradition

Often, when Virginian communities gathered for communal meals and fellowship in colonial and Federal eras, hosts expected invitees to bring their own eating utensils such as a cup, a knife and a spoon. An advertisement for a Virginia-style barbecue held in Augusta, Georgia, in 1840 illustrates that fact: "The Barbecue today, will be strictly after the old Virginia style, in the olden time, those therefore who intend to participate should not go unprovided with a knife, with which to, 'cut their way,' into the delicious legs of mutton &c., which will be served for the occasion."[3] "In the olden time" refers to when Virginia was on the colonial frontier and those who attended soups and barbecues brought their own eating utensils to the events, often consisting of a hunting knife, one tin cup and a single spoon.

Waste Not, Want Not

Being able to make the most out of available food has always been an important human skill. Although not as popular in our times, in the past animal heads, feet and offal were common foods eaten by Americans, especially by the less well-to-do and enslaved people. During the Civil War, fresh meat was scarce in Virginia. On the rare occasions that some families acquired meats, they were often no more than offal or the head of a carcass. Cooks made the best of them by cooking soup, stew or hash.[4] When my father's family and friends slaughtered hogs during the Great Depression, they served the fresh liver and lights for their hog killing day breakfast. Others used those parts to make hash. In fact, hash was a perfect side dish for barbecues when thrifty cooks slaughtered animals and barbecued them whole in times before refrigeration. It makes perfect sense that the nutritious parts of freshly slaughtered animals that were not well suited for barbecuing, such as scraps of meat and offal, became ingredients used to make hash.

Hash: A Love-Hate Relationship

Of all the barbecue stews, barbecue hash (which is hash served at barbecues or with barbecue sauce in it) presents the greatest puzzle to the eater. Recipes include various meats, offal and vegetables that the cook chops and cooks down to almost a mush.[5] Some scratch their heads when presented with the "mysterious preparation." Others describe barbecue hash as a "smooth meat puree."[6] Advice for making hash in 1897 includes the instruction "add a little water and stew to make a mush—that's hash."[7] In 1911, a writer for the *Edgefield Advertiser* commented on the word *hash*, "There is no definition for this word—nobody knows what hash is."[8] Another author commented, "It takes a great deal of confidence to really enjoy any kind of hash."[9] Such statements may explain the warning issued in 1831 that "hashing is a mode of cookery by no means suited to delicate stomachs."[10] That may be a reference to how hash inspires people to imagine the worst when eating it, which prompted the old saying, "Hash is like Faith, the substance of things hoped for, the evidence of things not seen."[11]

In the nineteenth century, patrons gave restaurants and hotels that served hash the unflattering name "hash houses." Because of hash's bad reputation in the nineteenth century, people tried to disguise it by giving it more appetizing names. If served in a dish, some called it "mince." If served in the shape of cakes, some called it "Fricandelles." When made into balls, people called it "croquettes." When baked in pastry, it was simply "pie." The cookbook *How to Cook Well*, published in 1886, has a recipe for hash unabashedly called "hidden hash."[12]

Regardless of whether people loved it or hated it, hash was popular because it was a way of using offal and leftover foods in order to prevent waste.[13] This is why the duke of Wellington called hash "[w]hat is left from the fight of yesterday."[14] In 1886, Margaret Arthur alluded to the importance of hash as a way to make the most of food resources when she wrote in *Good Housekeeping* that hash had "done more to advance the human race than any other mixed food."[15] A poet captured this aspect of hash in 1847:

> *Now listen all ye matrons, who would save your husband's cash,*
> *And are willing on a washing day to dine on savoury hash,*
> *And save yourselves the trouble of roasting, and of boiling,*
> *And the fear that each and every dish is in the course of spoiling;*
> *I'll teach how, by wise economy, you may save your scraps of meat*
> *That are left from plenteous dinners, and make a hash complete.*[16]

Because people rarely knew what was in their plate of hash, it was said that "one knows, or thinks he knows, that leftover meat and onions make hash; whatever else may be in it one eats it on faith."[17] The old slang expression "to make a hash" also illustrates that fact—it was another way of saying "to make a mess."[18] In 1880, John M. Dagnall, the author

A Virginia Tradition

Dukes Barbecue in Charleston, South Carolina, serves hash on its buffet. *Author's collection.*

of *Our American Hash*, recorded his thoughts on the dish in satire and verse.[19] Dagnall wrote of how a fictitious artist living in "Hashville" named Quill Chromo "sacrificed his dignity to the delectable luxury of hash." He complained, "Isn't it a shame to impose on the stomach with Hash!" He then went on to explain that eating hash makes people weak, dull and dimwitted. Hash, according to Chromo, is even responsible for unscrupulous politicians. Explaining how hash is "the poet's enemy," he wrote:

> *No, no, bid me ne'er again on vile Hash dine,*
> *Nor it devour at breakfast nor at supper;*
> *May dead my sense of smell be at the time;*
> *My nose ne'er again lead me thus to suffer.*

In 1886, *Puck* magazine published an article titled, "Confessions of a Hash-Eater." In it, the author wrote about "the miseries" that he experienced from eating hash. He expounded on how his "whole philosophy of life became colored by hash fancies." He went on to describe how just about everything reminded him of the dreadful hash. His hash malady even made him imagine that the universe itself was made of hash, as he wrote, "For, do I not know that however good or great you may be, you are still only an infinitesimal atom in the great universe of hash?"[20]

Onions to the Rescue

In 1890, a writer observed that Georgia-style barbecue hash is "delicately redolent of onions."[21] South Carolina–style hash also includes a generous amount of onions. In 1889, an author wrote about the delightful "big washpots of onion-scented hash" served at South Carolina barbecues.[22] Some South Carolina hash masters use at least an equal amount, by weight, of onions and meat in their barbecue hash. This practice is a holdover from past times when cooks believed that "a liberal allowance of minced onions" could "disguise anything objectionable."[23]

On the rare occasions that plantation owners gave a steer, lamb or hog to enslaved people that they could slaughter for a barbecue, the cooks used the head, offal, trotters (pig's feet) and scraps of meat to make barbecue hash.[24] While the carcass was barbecuing, hash masters put scraps of meat and the offal into large pots and stewed them for so long that they were no longer identifiable. The hash was highly seasoned with onions, salt and red pepper. Even though it had humble beginnings, over time barbecue hash was elevated to a prominent place at barbecues and other outdoor festivals,

Home Team BBQ in Charleston, South Carolina, serves a traditional barbecue hash made with liver. *Author's collection.*

reaching its peak of popularity after the end of the Civil War. The use of "giblets" to make barbecue hash is in keeping with the purpose of the dish, which is to prevent waste, and explains why some today still refer to barbecue hash as "liver hash."[25]

Native Americans and Hash

Several authors recorded how Native Americans made hash in times past. James Smith (1737–1813) was a frontiersman and eventually a legislator in the Kentucky General Assembly. In 1755, during his time on the frontier, Native Americans took him captive. Years later, he wrote of a great feast held by his captors that consisted of "a huge kettle of boiled corn and hashed venison."[26] James Mooney (1861–1921), who lived for several years among the Cherokee Indians, told how Sioux Indians pounded dried meat into hash with a stone hammer before making a stew with it.[27] John Lawson (1674–1711), an English explorer, described the hospitality shown to him by Native Americans. Although not called hash in the account, it's clear that hash is what his hosts served: "[They] made us very welcome with fat barbecu'd Venison, which the Woman of the Cabin took and tore in Pieces with her Teeth, so put it into a Mortar, beating it to Rags, afterwards stews it with Water, and other Ingredients, which makes a very savoury Dish."[28]

Father Pierre-Jean de Smet (1801–1873), a Belgian Roman Catholic missionary who worked with Native Americans in the midwestern and western United States, wrote about what he called "Rocky Mountain hash." He described the unappetizing way that Native Americans in that part of the country prepared it in kettles: "Often half a dozen women are occupied for hours preparing this rare stew. They chew and chew again mouthful after mouthful, then put the whole in the kettle. This is the far-famed Rocky Mountain hash!"[29]

Barbecue Hash in the United States

Although it is mainly found in South Carolina today, up until the end of World War II barbecue hash, in one form or another, was cooked all over the United States. In 1852, hosts of the Slash Cottage Barbecue held near

Richmond, Virginia, served "pig's head hash" with the barbecued meats. In 1855, the hosts of a barbecue held in Fredericksburg, Virginia, served "shoat hind hash." There was so much food served at that barbecue that it took twelve cooks working for two days to prepare the food and 150 waiters to serve all of it. In the 1920s, barbecue hash was a specialty of the Park Springs Hotel in Danville, Virginia.[30]

Virginians have also served their fair share of hidden hash masquerading as barbecue. The cookbook *Virginia Cookery Past and Present*, published in 1957, includes a recipe titled "Barbecue Filling for Buns." It is actually a Virginia-style barbecue hash recipe disguised as barbecue. Churches served sandwiches made with the barbecue hash to raise funds for their ministries.[31] Old 1950s and 1960s advertisements for James River Brand Smithfield Barbecue, no longer commercially available, describe another way Virginians served barbecue hash. Those old advertisements depict the cook ladling barbecue out of a large iron kettle while describing the "rich and tender meat, tangy with barbecue sauce" that had been "lovingly simmered in old fashioned open kettles." Even though the Smithfield Ham and Products Company called sandwiches made with the tasty treat "barbecue sandwiches," the fact that the meat simmered with barbecue sauce in "open kettles" indicates that they were actually barbecue hash sandwiches. Clearly, the delicious product was another way that Virginians served "hidden hash." Years ago, in my hometown, it was common to find barbecue being sold that was composed of hashed barbecued meat and other ingredients cooked until it all was very soft before being mixed with barbecue sauce and served on hamburger buns. To this day, some of the old barbecue businesses in and around Richmond still serve those kinds of delicious Virginia-style hashed barbecue sandwiches.

People in North Carolina, Arizona and Texas used to make barbecue hash, too.[32] Old newspapers from the Tar Heel State have numerous advertisements in them for barbecue hash. For several decades, the people of Tryon, North Carolina, have hosted a barbecue hash contest. Many contestants make their hash with leftover barbecued meats. However, there are still people there who say that it is "almost brazen" to serve barbecue hash in North Carolina.[33]

In 1902, news reports blamed the death of Confederate veteran Alfred Hobgood on barbecue hash. While in Dallas attending the United Confederate Veterans Reunion, he sat down to enjoy a dish of Texas-style barbecue hash. Eating heartily, he inadvertently swallowed the brass tip from a shoestring that had made its way into his serving of hash. It poisoned

A Virginia Tradition

Virginia-style tangy "hashed" barbecue sandwich. *Author's collection*.

him, and he died a few days later.³⁴ Georgians embraced hash almost as strongly as they did Brunswick stew.³⁵ From 1884 we find, "The hospitality of Georgians is only surpassed by their roast shoat and barbecue hash."³⁶ In 1887, Georgians were claiming that anyone "is a fool" if they attempt to give a barbecue without "giblet hash."³⁷ Georgian hash masters have included milk, liver, kidneys, lights, beef and lamb in some of their versions of barbecue hash. They also served it with boiled chitterlings.³⁸

The 1886 cookbook *How to Cook Well* contains several American recipes for hash. One of them calls for mincing leftover meat after cooking it in a liquid such as stock or gravy. If there isn't enough meat for an entire meal, the recipe calls for adding potatoes.³⁹ One of the oldest plantation recipes recorded in *Two Centuries of Virginia Cooking* is a hash recipe made with mutton. The book also records a beef hash recipe.⁴⁰

Mary Randolph's 1824 cookbook, *The Virginia Housewife*, has two recipes that the author specifically called hash. One is "To Hash Beef." The other, "To Hash a Calf's Head," specifies sweetbreads as an optional ingredient. Randolph also shared several other recipes that include hidden hash. For example, her "Calf's Heart Recipe" includes a hash made with "lights" as a component of the dish. Her recipe "To Dress Lamb's Head and Feet" is clearly a hash recipe. It calls for boiling and mincing the tongue and heart along with the lamb meat. Randolph's "Shote's Head" recipe calls for boiling the young pig's head, brains and feet until they are "quite tender" before mincing them and serving the hash as a sauce with the pig's heart and liver. Her roast pig recipe calls for finely chopping the liver and using it in stuffing for the pig. After the pig is completely cooked, the recipe instructs the reader to remove the stuffing and mix it with wine to make a sauce. The dinner host was to serve this liver hash recipe over the pork just as South Carolinians and Georgians use barbecue hash as a sauce for barbecued pork. Randolph's recipe "To Barbecue Shote" calls for a barbecue sauce made with "forcemeat" mixed with wine, mushroom ketchup and seasonings. Randolph's forcemeat sauce is a hidden barbecue hash made of hashed meats mixed with suet and seasonings.

Fourth of July Barbecue, 1855
In 1855, the People of Fredericksburg and the surrounding counties held a Fourth of July barbecue. So much food was served that it required 12 cooks working two days to prepare it and 150 waiters to serve it. The bill of fare illustrates why Virginia barbecues were so famous.

8 Saddles Mutton	16 Fore Quarters Mutton	20 Roasted [barbecued] pigs
32 Quarters of Shoat	8 Shoat Hind Hashed and Stewed	26 Fore Quarters of Lamb
20 Hind Quarters of Lamb	500 Chickens	16 Quarters of Veal
4 Veal Heads—Stewed	30 Hams of Bacon	20 Pieces of Beef (10 lbs. each)
750 Loaves of Bread	6 lbs. Black Pepper	50 lbs. Lard
60 lbs. Butter	10 Bushels Potatoes	6 Bushels Beets
5 Bushels Onions	320 Heads of Cabbage	10 Gallons of Vinegar
120 lbs. Crushed Sugar	1 Gallon Currant Jelly	3 lbs. Mustard
1 Gallon Sweet Oil	2 Boxes Lemons	150 Quarts Wine
40 Gallons Whiskey	14 Bottles Brown Stout	6000 Feet of Lumber for Tables

Source: *Fredericksburg Herald,* July 9, 1855.

Lettice Bryan's 1839 cookbook, *The Kentucky Housewife*, has several hash recipes in it. Many of them call for onions and cream, among other ingredients. Bryan recommended toasted bread as an accompaniment.

In her "Shoat Cheese" recipe, Bryan states, "Shoat's head and feet make excellent hash when boiled tender, minced, and seasoned with butter, cream, flour and onions." Her "To Hash Beef" recipe calls for potatoes and cream. "To Hash a Knuckle of Veal" is prepared by boiling the meat until it is tender and adding butter, lemon zest and flour as a thickener. She suggests serving vinegar with it as a condiment. The "To Hash Calves' Feet" recipe also includes vinegar. The recipe "To Hash a Calf's Head" is very similar to the calf's head hash recipe in Mary Randolph's cookbook. Bryan's "Hashed Shoat" recipe calls for bread to thicken the hash. The recipe "To Bake a Pig" includes a sauce recipe that is actually a hidden hash served as a sauce. Bryan instructs us to "boil the feet, heart and liver, mince them fine, put them in a sauce-pan, with enough of the liquor in which they were boiled to make the gravy; add a small lump of butter, rolled in flour, a spoonful of sifted sage, a teaspoonful of pepper, a grated nutmeg, a handful of chopped parsley, and a glass of sweet cream; give it one boil and serve it up." Clearly, the sauce recipe made with feet, liver, cream, herbs and spices is a hash recipe. Again, this is similar to how Georgians made barbecue hash with cream or milk in it.

In the 1750s, Philadelphia shopkeeper Elizabeth Coates Paschall recorded the following barbecue recipe titled "To BarbeCue a Pig" in her book of receipts.[41] Although Paschall did not call it hash, the sauce for the barbecued pork is clearly a hidden barbecue hash recipe. Similar recipes in Randolph's and Bryan's cookbooks and others imply that using minced offal to make sauce for roasted and barbecued pork was a common practice. Paschall's recipe is as follows:

> *When it is fresh Killd & Neatly Cleand Slitt it open & Chine the back bone through to the outer skin Cutt out the Gristles from the Nose and the Inside Nastiness of the Ears: & pick & Clean the Brains & Season the pigg well with Coyan [cayenne] peper & Salt: & Lay him over Slow Coals on a BarbeCue Grid Iron till he is Done Enough with the Inside Downwards first but Don't Baste it at all for that Spoyle them till you turn the Skin Side down then only pour about a Small Glass of wine over the upper Side: & for Sauce Boyl the Liver Nott above a quarter of an hour butt the Lights & hart & pettetoes [feet] take as Long Doing as the pig & putt 4 or 5 Small Onions Chopt fine in it with them which must be Done as Long as they then pick the Liver & Lights Clean from the arteries & veins that are in them Chop them very fine & the Brains that were boyled with them & with a Spoon take all the Gravey & wine of the pig & putt*

in the Sauce & bruise the Liver & brains with the back of a Spoon very fine & putt as Much of the Liquor they were boyld in as makes the sauce thin Enough & the onions with it if you Like them & Just give it a boyl up after you have Seasoned it to your Pallate with Salt & Coyan [cayenne]*: Civer your Pig with a Large tin Driping pan while he Does.*

Although unappetizing by modern standards, the portion of the recipe that explains how to make barbecue sauce with the feet, liver, lights, heart and brains is clearly a barbecue hash recipe.

By the 1940s, barbecue hash recipes were showing up in newspapers all across the United States. The recipes were a backyard barbecue twist on the hash recipes that thrifty cooks prepared for their families made with leftover meats. Such recipes were particularly important during World War II because of shortages and rationing. One World War II–era recipe calls for using leftover veal. To that was added ketchup, vinegar, mustard and brown sugar. Other similar recipes call for leftover meats mixed with ingredients such as barbecue sauce or chili sauce. Some recipes called for serving the hash over rice or for adding potatoes, which increased the quantity of hash needed to feed larger families.[42]

In 1954, the U.S. Department of Agriculture published a barbecue hash recipe for serving twenty-five to one hundred people. Ingredients include "cooked beef," "cooked potatoes," onions, green peppers, chili sauce, chili pepper, ketchup and Worcestershire sauce. After the onions and peppers are sautéed, the recipe instructs us to bake the hash for one hour and ten minutes.[43]

South Carolina Barbecue Hash

South Carolinians still cherish their barbecue hash tradition. As one South Carolinian put it in 1884, hash "is the all-important thing at a barbecue." That fact hasn't changed.[44] South Carolinians serve barbecue hash by itself, over bread, over rice, over grits, over barbecue or in hash sandwiches. All variations of barbecue hash in South Carolina share the same soft texture only achieved by long cooking.

Lowcountry barbecue hash found in the Charleston area might contain hogshead, chicken liver and/or pork liver. The Charleston version may also contain vegetables such as tomatoes, potatoes, bell peppers, carrots and onions,

Barbecue hash simmering at a barbecue in Augusta, Georgia, in 1866. Sketch by Theodore R. Davis from *Harper's Weekly*, November 10, 1866. *Author's collection.*

Barbecue hash made with beef is often served over bread rather than rice in the Upcountry region of South Carolina. *Author's collection.*

but you won't be able to tell by looking at it. Some there add barbecue sauce to it. People in the more northern and western regions around Spartanburg and Columbia do not generally add offal to their Upcountry barbecue hash. There it is made with beef or pork and is usually only seasoned with simple ingredients like salt, pepper, butter and red pepper.[45]

In addition to regional differences, there is also South Carolina barbecue hash made with pulled meat cooked so long that nothing is left of it except the individual meat fibers that resemble strings. South Carolinians call this type of hash "string hash."[46] Then there is the South Carolina barbecue hash that calls for ground meat. After the meat has cooked for hours and is tender, the hash master removes it from the pot and chops it or runs it through a meat grinder before returning it to the pot.[47] Similarly, some Brunswick stew and burgoo cooks allow the meat to remain in strings, while others prefer to chop or grind the meat after it is cooked. Native American stews also had the same styles. Sometimes they tore dried meat into shreds before adding it to the stew pot. At other times, they used stone tools to mince it.

Some South Carolinians have claimed that barbecue hash must be prepared in an iron kettle outside, uncovered, over an open fire. Another South Carolina tradition holds that the cook must prepare barbecue hash

Barbecue hash and rice at Swig & Swine BBQ in Charleston, South Carolina. *Author's collection.*

under the light of a full moon. In fact, there have been hash masters in South Carolina who would only sell hash on the last Saturday of the month in order to ensure that they cooked it under the greatest amount of moonlight.[48]

There are also some lesser-known barbecue hash cooking traditions. In the year 1919, a meat market in Greenwood, South Carolina, claimed that it served the "very best of barbecue hash fixed by experts" and encouraged customers to eat it because it was "prepared scientifically."[49] The "scientific" way of preparing hash may be a response to reforms that were sweeping the food industry after Upton Sinclair's 1906 book *The Jungle* sparked public outrage by exposing the unsanitary practices of that era's meatpacking industry. Campaigns waged by food companies to notify the public of their clean food-handling practices were all the rage. For example, in 1916, the Chicago-based Morris & Company was zealously advertising its way of canning barbecue hash with "absolute cleanliness" that was "a paramount rule." The purpose of such advertising campaigns was most likely to reassure consumers who were suspicious of the "mysterious preparation" especially after learning of the revelations in Sinclair's book.[50]

WILLIAM HAISLIP: A VIRGINIAN BARBECUE HASH MASTER

No self-respecting Virginian would dare put liver, heart, kidneys, lights, trotters or goozles in Brunswick stew or squirrel soup. Therefore, in the nineteenth century, Virginians cooked hash and/or Brunswick stew at barbecues and never confused the two. We find this fact illustrated in a remarkable story about a nineteenth-century Virginia barbecue cook named William Haislip who often cooked both a kettle of hash and a kettle of squirrel soup at his barbecues.

William Haislip was born in Hanover County, Virginia, in 1821. His friends called him "Black Hawk." He married Lucy Pierce in 1858 in Spotsylvania County, Virginia. Except for when he served in the Fifty-Fifth Virginia Infantry during the Civil War, Haislip continued to live there until his death in 1906. After the end of the Civil War, Haislip was often the master of ceremonies at large barbecues, eventually becoming a famous barbecue cook in and around Spotsylvania County. He was very proud of his skill at the pits and boasted that he was the "only man in the state competent to cook a whole ox properly."[51] In 1900, newspapers reported how Haislip visited President William McKinley in the White House in order to invite him to a Virginia barbecue. Haislip proudly spoke of his barbecued beef, his squirrel soup and his Virginia-style barbecue hash.[52] The *Philadelphia Inquirer*'s account of the event is as follows:

> *There was a unique visitor at the White House today, and contrary to the rules he was admitted to the private office of President McKinley. The visitor, who looked as though he were ready to invest in green goods or gold bricks, was William Haislup* [sic]*, a gray-haired Virginian with eighty years to his credit. The President enjoyed the visit of the old man immensely and is considering an invitation Mr. Haislup verbally extended him to attend a barbecue at Spottsylvania* [sic] *Court House in October. For Mr. Haislup is what is spoken of in the South as a "barbecuer" of the first water. To be able to cook a Southern barbecue means to obtain high distinction and to be loved by all.*
>
> *"I've bin cooking barbecues since I was a boy," said Mr. Haislup. "Four years ago, they paid me fer cooking an ox an' making squirrel soup at a barbecue fer that man Bryant, but I've come to like Mr. McKinley, and I'm going to vote for him. I've bin a Dimmycrat fer fifty or sixty years, but I never saw such a change in my life. All up through Spottsylvania ther people is changing, and McKinley will be our next President Sure. I think Spottsylvania will go Republican this time.*
>
> *"Did you never tend a barbecue? Well, we cook a whole ox over a coal fire, kill some sheep an' shoats an' cook them ther same way, an' make squirrel soup. Oh, yes, squirrel soup is mighty fine. Ther last big barbecue we had one hundred squirrels cut up in ther pot of soup. We put onions, pertaters an' lots of good things in ther soup. We takes some of ther meat from ther ox an' makes hash.*
>
> *"I jest knows that if ther President comes down to Spottsylvania to our barbecue he'll eat ther finest grub he ever had in his life. I'm ther onlyest man in my county that can roast a whole ox, an' when ther President comes down I'm going to have ther fattest ox in ther State of Virginny."*

Chapter 5

BRUNSWICK STEW

We crossed the stream upon a shaking plank laid from bank to bank, and strolled down the slope to the scene of operations. An immense kettle was swung over a fire of logs that were so many living coals. The smell of Brunswick stew had been wafted to us while we leaned on the fence. A young man, who had the reputation of being an epicure, to the best of his knowledge and ability, superintended the manufacture of the famous delicacy. "Two dozen chickens went into it!" he assured us. "They wanted to make me think it couldn't be made without green corn and fresh tomatoes. I knew a trick worth two of that. I have worked it before with dried tomatoes and dried sweet corn soaked overnight." He smacked his lips and winked fatuously.
—Marion Harland, Autobiography: The Story of a Long Life, *1910*

American author Mary Virginia Terhune was born in Amelia County, Virginia, in 1830. Her pen name was Marion Harland, under which she authored several books. She lived to the ripe old age of ninety-one. In her autobiography, she vividly described a Virginia barbecue held near Powhatan, Virginia, in 1844.[1] The enticing aromas of barbecuing meats and Brunswick stew made with a perfectly seasoned mix of meat, tomatoes, potatoes, corn and butterbeans filled the air. The pit masters tending the barbecue pits and the stew masters constantly stirring simmering pots of Brunswick stew entertained and tantalized the hungry crowd as they eagerly waited to partake of the feast. Such events were frequent during the months of May through October in nineteenth-century Virginia.

Virginia's Brunswick stew recipe, declared "a gastronomic triumph" by newspaper reporters, has stood the test of time.² Over the centuries, some have even compared it to the stew that Jacob used to tempt his brother Esau. In 1905, a lover of the stew suggested that we should have great sympathy for Esau simply because no one can resist the savory stew.³ Others have expressed pity for anyone who hasn't tasted the mouthwatering delicacy. In 1903, a writer described his "deep regret" that "millions of good people have been born, walked and fretted their allotted time upon earth, and died without the happiness of having eaten of a dish of it."⁴ The sympathy for those who have never enjoyed a bowl of Brunswick stew may be rooted in this claim made in 1926: "After a dinner of Brunswick stew you will have a song on your lips and a smile of oceanic expansion, and if your youth has departed, it will return."⁵ American poet and native-born Virginian John Bannister Tabb (1845–1909) expressed his tender affection for Brunswick stew in a poem titled "The Tryst":

> *Potato was deep in dark underground,*
> *Tomato, above in the light.*
> *The little Tomato was ruddy and round,*
> *The little Potato was white.*
> *And redder and redder she rounded above,*
> *And paler and paler he grew,*
> *And neither suspected a mutual love*
> *Till they met in a Brunswick Stew.*

In nineteenth-century Virginia, the Brunswick stew season started in March or April and continued into the late fall. It went into full swing in August, which is harvest time for what's called "the Virginia trinity," comprising corn, butterbeans and tomatoes.⁶ Still today, Virginia's Brunswick stew and barbecue traditions live on. People all over Virginia get together to hold a "Brunswick stew" (some call it simply "a stew"), where family and friends enjoy the delicious dish cooked outside in a large kettle or pot.⁷ Moreover, charity organizations have learned that Brunswick stew is a very popular and effective way to raise money for good causes. In fact, some regions in Virginia nicknamed Brunswick stew "church-builder chicken."⁸ Many Virginia barbecue restaurants still serve it because it remains a perfect side dish for Virginia-style barbecue. Recognizing that fact, a writer for the *Evening News* commented in 1905 that without Brunswick stew "a Virginia barbecue would not be complete."⁹

A Virginia Tradition

Brunswick stew cooks at the historic Magnolia Grange plantation house in Chesterfield, Virginia, circa 1925. *Courtesy Chesterfield Historical Society of Virginia.*

Over the last two hundred years, Brunswick stew became popular all throughout the United States, even as far south as Florida, north at least as far as Michigan and west as far as Texas and California. The fact that Brunswick stew masters have prepared the dish at barbecues and other public gatherings over the last two centuries is a monument to its timeless and universal appeal.

Just about every modern recipe for Brunswick stew calls for butterbeans, tomatoes and corn. After that, recipes vary. A Florida variety calls for beef, pork, chicken or mutton, and some add beef heart or pork heart.[10] A Tennessee version includes ham, like some southeastern Virginia recipes.[11] There is a Michigan version that includes beef shank.[12] A California version of Brunswick stew, noted as being "a Virginia dish," which is a nod to its Virginian origins, includes rice in the recipe, like some North Carolina versions of the stew.[13] Old Georgia versions call for milk and beef liver, and vegetables.[14] People who live in some parts of Appalachia use mutton, ground beef or ground pork in Brunswick stew. Some there also add ketchup or steak sauce to the recipe.[15] Kentuckians have cooked their share of Brunswick stew. They have even sold it by the bucket much like the famous

Quarts of Brunswick stew ready to be served. *Author's collection.*

chicken that bears their state's name. An advertisement in a 1908 edition of Kentucky's *Paducah Evening Sun* exhorted, "Bring your bucket and buy some of this delicious [Brunswick] stew."[16]

Brunswick Stew in Virginia

Frontiersmen and settlers in Virginia have eaten squirrel meat since the earliest days of the colony. John Smith wrote that Powhatan Indians introduced the colonists to dishes made with Virginian squirrels. Settlers often cooked the thin colonial and Federal-era squirrel soup in large iron pots over open fires seasoned with salt and red pepper. Red pepper—or "home-raised" pepper, as some called it—was popular because, unlike black pepper, settlers on the frontier could grow it. It was a cheap and readily available substitute for black pepper.[17] At some point, Virginians improved the squirrel soup by transforming it into a rich, hearty, hash-like stew. That set the stage for the birth of the dish we now call Brunswick stew.

A Virginia Tradition

Most Virginia-style Brunswick stew recipes call for butter, black pepper and red pepper regardless of the type of meat used. Virginia-style Brunswick stew must be rich and highly seasoned to make it "racy of the soul" (spicy), and generally, it should be thick rather than soupy.[18] In the past, people ate the stew while hot or cold, although nowadays people usually eat it while hot. When cold, a properly prepared Virginia Brunswick stew will have a consistency similar to headcheese.[19]

Virginia's Brunswick stew has created millions of fans over the last two hundred years. The stew is considered to be such an irresistible delicacy that Judge John Y. Mason (1799–1859) of Virginia traveled all the way to Europe in the mid-nineteenth century to introduce the stew to people in Paris, France.[20] Called the "Virginia dish that cannot be too highly recommended," Brunswick stew has been inspiring regional variations and heated stew feuds for more than a century.[21] Its "ambrosial" qualities—such as the rich broth, tender meats, tangy tomatoes and sweet corn—compel people in regions where it's popular to jealously claim it as their own.

Virginians have hallowed rules for making the stew, and disagreements over them have divided Virginia stew masters into several, for lack of a better phrase, "Virginia-style Brunswick stew sects." The original

Stirring forty gallons of Brunswick stew in Mechanicsville, Virginia. *Author's collection.*

Brunswick stew recipe requires squirrel meat and middling or bacon and onions, with bread crumbs to act as a thickener. In the 1830s, that changed when people discovered that potatoes, tomatoes, corn and butterbeans were delicious additions.[22] As Brunswick stew moved from plantations and farms to urban areas, squirrel meat became scarce. Therefore, the recipe changed to allow for chicken, beef, veal, pork, rabbit or lamb. Alternatively, you can include several types of meat in the same pot.[23]

During World War II, veal became a popular choice in Virginia for Brunswick stew because, unlike chicken, it wasn't as susceptible to frequent shortages.[24] There is an old recipe from Hampton, Virginia, that calls for a mix of veal, beef and chicken.[25] Another Virginia recipe, published in 1941, calls for a "veal shin" and a whole chicken.[26] A version of Brunswick stew from Buckingham County, Virginia, includes fatback, beef fat, pork and turkey, as well as carrots, cabbage, garlic and bell peppers.[27] A Brunswick stew recipe from Farmville, Virginia, specifies mashed potatoes.[28] Traditionally, potatoes in Virginia's Brunswick stew cook so long that they disintegrate into it, acting as a thickener. Adding precooked mashed potatoes serves as a time-saving step. Speaking of potatoes and variations, folks in Millers Tavern, Virginia, make a thick Brunswick stew using white potatoes, sweet potatoes and carrots in addition to meats such as chicken, beef, bacon and veal.[29] Other unique Virginian versions of Brunswick stew only contain either smoked pork, fresh spare ribs or fatback. Although the use of butterbeans is strongly encouraged, neither they nor potatoes are always required in Virginian versions of the stew.[30]

Controversial ingredients (at least among Virginians) such as peas, okra, garlic, wine and Worcestershire sauce show up in some Virginia recipes. In 1903, a reporter for the *Richmond Times-Dispatch* was excited about the start of the "Brunswick stew season." He enthusiastically described the stew served in and around Richmond that contained all kinds of vegetables including an unusual ingredient in Virginia-style Brunswick stew: peas.[31]

The Brunswick stew recipe printed in the 1885 edition of the *Virginia Cookery-Book* explained that it should be "cooked until the ingredients of which it is made cannot be distinguished the one from the other." The recipe includes the typical Virginia Brunswick stew ingredients, with the addition of nontraditional ingredients such as a cucumber, squash, a carrot and okra, along with the note that you can add "some of every vegetable that you can get, except rice—there must be none of that."[32] Most Virginia stew masters would agree that rice shouldn't be a part of the recipe. However, most would disagree with the claim that "some of every vegetable you can get" is allowed in Brunswick stew.

Soon after Virginia's Reconstruction era, R.T.W. Duke Sr. incorporated both Worcestershire sauce and okra in his Virginia-style Brunswick stew recipe.[33] Some Virginians have even added a little sherry to the recipe from time to time.[34] However, such additions to the stew recipe can cause distress among traditionalists, who often consider such ingredients "heresy." Virginian W.H. Boyle wrote to the editor of the *Richmond Times-Dispatch* in 1946 because he was "distressed" over a recipe for Brunswick stew distributed by the Richmond Chamber of Commerce. Living in Atlanta, Georgia, at the time, Boyle recounted a description of the Brunswick stew served at local restaurants in Atlanta as "a slopping plate of coarse canned corn and tomatoes boiled with a handful of hamburger meat." Boyle added that it

---

Mrs. M.E. Brodnax, Rux, Virginia, to Dr. Taylor, Cochran, Virginia, May 6, 1907

My brother, Robert, has brought me your letter asking about the origin of "the Brunswick stew." It was first made by an old man—a retainer of Dr. Creed Haskins, who lived at Mount Donum, on the banks of the Nottoway River. This old man, James Matthews—"Uncle Jimmy," as everybody called him—was a good cook and an inveterate hunter, particularly of squirrels. He always killed the squirrels and made "the stew" at picnics and public gatherings as long as he lived—and delighted to do it. After his death Dr. Aaron Haskins succeeded him; and Cousin Jack Stith was his successor. After Jack Stith moved away the office descended to Col. W.T. Mason (Colonel Tom), whose stews were enjoyed throughout Red Oak for years. Old Uncle Jimmy Matthews made his reputation for good "stews" about 1828. The original stew was made with squirrels, butter, onions, stale bread and condiments. The addition of tomatoes and other vegetables finally became customary, but they were never a part of old Uncle Jimmy's stews. It is difficult for people to learn how to make the stew as originally made. Only experience can perfect one in cooking and seasoning properly.

I.E. Spatig, *Brunswick County, Virginia: Information for the Homeseeker and Investor*, 1907

was "doused with Worcestershire sauce until you could not tell what was in it except by looking." He went on to explain, "Brunswick stew is a [country] dish," and those "city touches do not belong in it." Boyle concluded that the Richmond Chamber of Commerce was destroying "the glory of Brunswick stew" by "disseminating a recipe that includes Worcestershire sauce," wine, cabbage, tomato puree and celery.[35] The writer of a letter written to the *Richmond Dispatch* in 1891 supports Boyle's assessment of "city" stew, writing that Brunswick stew "made according to the usual city formula is an unmitigated fraud and humbug."[36]

Marion Cabell Tyree's (1826–1912) cookbook *Housekeeping in Old Virginia*, published in 1879, contains several recipes for Virginia-style Brunswick stew. Tyree was Patrick Henry's granddaughter. Her cookbook is a compilation of recipes shared by nearly 250 Virginian women. One Brunswick stew recipe in Tyree's cookbook calls for boiling and mashing potatoes before putting them into the pot. Various meats are called for in the different recipes, including squirrel, chicken, "a twenty-five cent beef shank," middling and bacon.[37] In a 1905 cookbook titled *The Way to the Heart: A Collection of Tested Virginia Recipes*, written by Carrie Pickett Moore of Bon Air, Virginia, there is a recipe for Virginia-style Brunswick stew that doesn't call for salt or black or red pepper. However, it does specify bacon rather than fatback and Worcestershire sauce added just before serving.[38] A similar Virginia recipe titled "Chicken Brunswick Stew," published in 1941, prescribes "bacon drippings," and it, too, omits the salt, black pepper and red pepper.[39] However, based on the majority of recipes, salt, black pepper and red pepper are ubiquitous ingredients in Virginia-style Brunswick stew, and one wonders if the authors simply neglected to mention them.

The most popular meats used in Virginia Brunswick stew nowadays are bacon or middling (other names for it include fatback, salt pork or white meat) with chicken. Most Virginia cooks chop the pork before adding it to the pot, and some chop the other meats in Brunswick stew after they are tender and return them to the pot.[40] Generally, the proper Virginia version continues to cook until the meat turns to shreds, the beans are very soft and many if not all of the potatoes have melted into the stew.[41] The meats in a properly made kettle of Brunswick stew should have a similar consistency to barbecue hash. In 1891, readers of the *Richmond Dispatch* were instructed, "The stew ought to have a liberal quantity of meat and be boiled down to a thick consistency, or until but little liquid is left in it."[42] Moore wrote in her cookbook, "The secret of a good Brunswick stew is long, slow boiling." The long simmer results in many of the ingredients becoming very soft and almost disappearing into the stew. Another recipe for Virginia-style Brunswick stew, published in 1894, instructs the reader, "When properly made no one is able to detect any of the ingredients."[43] This description of a hash-like Brunswick stew is slightly overstated when it comes to a proper Virginia-style Brunswick stew, but not by much. The butterbeans are usually identifiable, and so is the corn unless cream-style corn is used.

Although most Virginians agree that Brunswick stew must simmer for a long time, there is some disagreement over the consistency of the corn used in the dish. In an effort to correct the errors of city dwellers in Richmond, Virginia, in 1891, a stew enthusiast admonished them, writing, "Canned corn should never be used."[44] A recipe in *Housekeeping in Old Virginia* calls for the corn to be grated. Some cooks used to split the corn kernels with a knife before cutting them off the cob. Others simply scraped the corn kernels off the cob before putting them in the pot. These techniques ensure that the corn melts into the stew after long cooking. The starchy liquid from the corn kernels helps to thicken the stew. Nowadays, instead of scraping or splitting the corn kernels, some Virginia stew masters use cream-style corn.[45] In spite of that, others in Virginia prefer the texture of the corn in Brunswick stew to be crisp. Cooks accomplish this by adding whole corn kernels no more than thirty minutes before serving.

Now, before someone decides to chop the meat while cooking Brunswick stew, they need to first consider the fact that some in Virginia won't stand for it. There are Virginia Brunswick stew cooks who hold that meat should only be pulled from the bones and then pulled into shreds before returning it to the pot. Under no circumstances should anyone ever cut the meat in any way when removing it from the bones of the carcass. With this technique, where the meat is "pulled" rather than being chopped, the individual meat fibers cook down into what stew cooks call "strings." There are versions of barbecue hash and burgoo that also share this characteristic. Mrs. Thomas Thweatt, "born and reared in Brunswick County," shared these instructions in 1947. Referring to the Brunswick stew pot monument that Georgians erected in 1946, she wrote, "It amuses me when other places try so hard to get the credit for the origin of this delectable dish." She continued, "I get the big laugh when they begin to indicate the vegetables that go in it." She was a purist when it came to Brunswick stew and held to the original recipe. According to her, the stew "has not one vegetable in it except onion." She explained, "Vegetable stew is good, I grant you, but it is not Brunswick stew." Moreover, the only acceptable meats are squirrel or lamb unless you are cooking at home in your kitchen. In that case, chicken is acceptable. The only acceptable seasonings for Brunswick stew are butter, salt, black pepper and red pepper. Her preferred way of thickening the stew was with bread. When served on a plate, Mrs. Thweatt wrote, "We like it thick." When served in a bowl, it "should be thinner."[46]

Although not traditional, some in Virginia use leftover meats in their Brunswick stew. Some restaurants there even use leftover barbecued pork or barbecued chicken. I have a good guess that Mrs. Thweatt would be horrified at such a thing. Perhaps all of us should be. Leftover meats go into hash, not Virginia-style Brunswick stew.

Brunswick Stew in Texas

People in Texas have served Brunswick stew from time to time.[47] People there make a version of it according to the basic Virginia-style recipe that contains chicken. However, some there took to calling it "Hopkins County stew." Described as the "sweetest poetry" and the "loveliest flowers stirred with a magic spoon and blended until it transforms into the soothing influence of song," Hopkins County stew is certainly another one of the Lone Star state's culinary achievements, even if its contribution to it was just giving it a Texas name.[48] Texans have cooked Hopkins County stew since at least the late nineteenth century in and around the city of Sulphur Springs in Hopkins County, Texas.[49] The recipe includes potatoes, tomatoes, corn, bacon, chicken, chili pepper pods and salt. Originally made with squirrel just like the Virginia version, nowadays it often includes beef or fowl.[50]

Brunswick Stew in North Carolina

Brunswick stew is very popular in North Carolina. People in Brunswick, North Carolina, have even made claims that it originated there. However, there was a time when some North Carolinians felt the need to rename it "corn muddle." The basic recipe for corn muddle is the same as Virginia's Brunswick stew recipe, with the exception that it may include any available small game. Unlike Virginia's version, squirrel isn't required and never was the first meat of choice for the stew in that state.[51] In 1954, a columnist for the *Greensboro Daily News* declared that Brunswick stew only attains its "finest flowering" in eastern North Carolina. The stew, according to the writer, is "far beyond the capabilities of the residents" of Virginia, and a Tennessean "hardly understands food to begin with." The debauchery of West Virginians' cuisine is testified to by the large amount of money they spend on canned soup. True North Carolina–style Brunswick stew, the writer asserted, "just happens." There is no recipe for it. The cook uses whatever ingredients are on hand, be it fresh or leftover. Above all, the cook "must simply not give a hoot," and the stew must not be "hurried along." There is no need to stir it. After the ingredients are put in the pot on the stove, it's time to go sit on the front porch. Only when the cook reluctantly rises from his or her nap, roused by hunger or the smell of smoke, is the stew done. The author concluded by explaining that the finest Brunswick stew in history will "one day be prepared by a catatonic cook." Therefore, to cook North Carolina–style Brunswick stew, you must observe two words: "Relax yourself."[52]

Brunswick Stew in Georgia

Georgians love Brunswick stew as much as any people in the South and have for a long time. In fact, they have long considered Brunswick stew to be a "necessary adjunct of a first-class barbecue."[53] In 1909, President Taft couldn't resist the Georgia version of Brunswick stew served to him in Atlanta along with that other Georgia favorite, "'possum and taters."[54] Brunswick stew is so popular in Georgia that Georgians are convinced that they must have invented it. In addition to versions of Georgia-style Brunswick stew that are similar to Virginia's version, some Georgian versions of the stew reflect a uniquely Georgian twist.

Like Virginians, Georgians are dogmatic about what constitutes "real" Brunswick stew. During the observation of "Georgia Week" in 1946, a Washington, D.C., restaurant served what it billed as "Brunswick stew." The stew wasn't authentic. Congressional representatives from Georgia were outraged. One complained, "I wish you could have seen the mess they were serving under that sacred name! It might as well have been creamed chicken, with a few pieces of liver and lamb and a scattering of green peas."[55] Such reactions help explain why it is said that "Brunswick stew is as important to a genuine Georgia pit barbecue as is the bride to

Brunswick stew being cooked at a barbecue in Atlanta, Georgia, in 1898. From *Strand Magazine*, October 1898. *Author's collection.*

a lovely garden wedding."⁵⁶ In 1894, a visitor to Georgia from a northern state related this account of his first Georgia barbecue:

> *You take a piece of plain bread. The meat is carried around in great bowls. You hold out a piece of bread. The man who carries the bowl of meat gracefully flicks a chunk of meat upon the bread. Another attendant usually is near with what is called "Brunswick stew." It is a mysterious compound whose ingredients I tried to discover, but without success. It appears to be composed of green corn, tomatoes, and red pepper, but I don't know. I do know that it is very good. A spoonful of Brunswick stew is ladled out upon the chunk of meat; then another slice of bread, a good, thick slice—none of your fashionable afternoon tea kind—is laid upon the whole. You give them a little squeeze to keep them together and begin to bite.*⁵⁷

Some versions of Georgia's Brunswick stew are actually barbecue hash and Brunswick stew hybrids. Consider the previous accounts of Georgia-style Brunswick stew. First, the poorly made stew served during "Georgia Week" in 1946 contained liver, which is a hash ingredient. Second, the waiter at the 1894 barbecue served the stew as a sauce on a barbecue sandwich, which is a hash-like use of the stew. These details reveal the fat that some Georgians have served hidden hash masquerading as Brunswick stew. A Virginian living in Georgia in 1946 noticed this fact. He wrote to the *Richmond Times-Dispatch* about Georgia-style Brunswick stew, "[T]he local concoction is not a stew but a moist hash."[58]

As mentioned earlier, some recipes for Georgian-style Brunswick stew call for milk and liver.[59] An 1897 edition of the *American Kitchen Magazine* described Georgia-style Brunswick stew as a "celebrated dish" made with liver, tongues, heads and tails (and so on) of "the barbecued meats." Added to the meats were "a generous seasoning of peppers, salt, sweet herbs and vegetables." After boiling it until "it is smooth," guests ate it by itself or it was "used as sauce for the meats."[60] This may explain why Georgians are so fond of the bizarre practice (from the viewpoint of a Virginian) of putting barbecue sauce in their Brunswick stew. At any rate, clearly Georgians combined hash with Brunswick stew and created their own version of the dish.

In 1920, an author for the *Macon Telegraph* compared and contrasted Georgia-style Brunswick stew with breakfast hash. Like breakfast hash, the author explained, people eat Brunswick stew even though they can't tell what's in it. In contrast to breakfast hash made with leftover meats, Georgia-style Brunswick stew included fresh ingredients such as "the haslet of the hog, the heart, liver, lights, kidneys, the goozle, [and] the head and feet of the hog."[61] Some Georgian versions also call for dairy products, which is similar to old cream hash recipes.[62] All of those are barbecue hash ingredients. In Virginia, where Brunswick stew originated, cooks have never put such ingredients in the stew, and while I suppose some Virginians have, using Brunswick stew as a sauce for barbecue sandwiches was never a widely observed custom in the Old Dominion.

A Georgia stew master revealed his "Brunswick stew" recipe in an 1895 account of a barbecue in Atlanta, Georgia. His instructions for cooking Georgia-style Brunswick stew are as follows: "Well, yer see, yer jest takes de meat, de hog's haid, an' de libbers, an' all sorts er little nice parts, an' yer chops it up wid corn an' permattuses, an' injuns, an' green peppers, an' yer stews and stews tell hit gits erlike, an' yer kain't tell what hit's made uv."[63]

That recipe makes it clear that either late nineteenth-century Georgia "stew dogs" (what some in Georgia call Brunswick stew masters) were serving hidden barbecue hash masquerading as Brunswick stew or they combined Virginia's Brunswick stew recipe with barbecue hash recipes to create the original version of Georgia-style Brunswick stew.

The Great Brunswick Stew Controversy

For well over a century, Brunswick stew enthusiasts have thought of the stew as "a dish fit for the gods." That explains why it was embroiled in the "Great Brunswick Stew Controversy" for more than one hundred years.[64] Brunswick stew is so irresistibly delicious that at least seven counties in Virginia alone have claimed to be its birthplace. There was even a heated dispute among the residents of Brunswick County, Virginia, about exactly where in that county it was first cooked. One faction claimed that people on the banks of the Meherrin River first cooked Brunswick stew. Another faction contended that people on the banks of the Nottoway River first cooked the stew.[65] However, that was just the beginning of the stew wars.

The controversy heated up sometime in the late nineteenth century, when "wordy wars" erupted. However, by 1903, the debate had pretty much been settled that Brunswick County, Virginia, was the original home of the stew.[66] Nevertheless, that period of peace didn't last long. The stew wars were not over, and the first to strike back were Georgians. In 1946, Georgians rekindled the debate by erecting a monument in Brunswick, Georgia, dedicated to, presumably, the first pot of Brunswick stew.[67] The monument is an iron kettle said to have come from a former slave ship named the *Wanderer* with an inscription proclaiming that people on nearby St. Simons Island cooked the first pot of Brunswick stew on July 2, 1898.[68]

In addition to arguing with Virginians over the origin of Brunswick stew, Georgians still argue about it among themselves. Some Georgians claim that a British sailor recorded the original recipe for Brunswick stew in 1728 while he was encamped near Brunswick, Georgia, on St. Simons Island.[69] However, according to them, it would be another forty-three years before the sailor's recipe for "a good and wholesome stew" would be cooked in Brunswick, Georgia, under the direction of General James Oglethorpe, the founder of the city, in 1771.[70]

Unsatisfied with the 1898 and 1771 origination theories, a third Georgian theory for the origin of Brunswick stew holds that followers of the Methodist evangelist John Wesley were the first to cook the stew using wild game and vegetables in Brunswick, Georgia, in the 1730s.[71] This appears to be the oldest Georgian claim for the origin of Brunswick stew.[72]

By 1988, it appears that some Georgians felt the need for yet another Brunswick stew origination claim. In that year, a Georgian placed a black kettle monument near the Georgia Welcome Center along Interstate 95.

A Virginia Tradition

The manufacturer made changes to labels on cans of James River Brand Smithfield Chicken Brunswick Stew over the years. The image on the left depicts pre-1980s cans. *Courtesy Isle of Wight County Museum. Used by permission.*

The inscription on the monument's plaque displays the claim that people "in the Brunswick Golden Isles area in early colonial days" were the first to cook Brunswick stew.

By 1844, and possibly as early as 1840, people in Virginia were cooking a stew they called "Brunswick stew."[73] The *National Cookery Book*, published in 1876, described Brunswick stew as "a well-known Virginia dish."[74] By 1886, twelve years before the date on the 1946 Georgia Brunswick stew monument, a Macon, Georgia newspaper printed an article that proclaimed Brunswick, Virginia, to be the origination place of Brunswick stew.[75] In 1887, the *Janesville Daily Gazette* claimed that Brunswick stew had a national reputation for being "the famous Virginia dish known as Brunswick stew."[76]

There is an advertisement in an 1871 edition of the *Savannah Daily Advisor* for "Old Virginia Brunswick Stew" being served at a local restaurant in Savannah, Georgia.[77] It is doubtful that a Georgia restaurant would serve the Virginia "copycat" version of the stew instead of the "original" Georgia version if it existed at that time.

As far back as 1867, A.P. Hill, a native-born Georgian, shared a recipe for Brunswick stew in her cookbook but didn't call it by that name. She called it "camp stew."[78] The Pulitzer Prize–winning author Marjorie Kinnan

Charlette Woolridge, Barbara Jarrett Harris, Barnard Jones Sr. and Nancy Watson were part of the stew crew in Richmond, Virginia, on Brunswick Stew Day in 2017. *Author's collection.*

Rawlings (1896–1953) visited Brunswick, Georgia, in 1942, hoping to sample the presumably original American version of Brunswick stew that she thought was brought to America from Braunschweig (aka Brunswick), Germany. She was surprised that she could find no one in that town who had ever heard of the dish. She wrote, "Lifted eyebrows greet a request for the dish in inns of that small city."[79] Going back even further, in 1862, a Georgia newspaper reprinted an article from the *Atlanta Confederacy* that included a recipe for "Virginia stew," which just so happens to describe the exact recipe for Virginia's Brunswick stew. The author quipped, "If, after a fair trial, you pronounce this an unpalatable dish, then your loyalty to the Southern Confederacy ought to be questioned."[80] In contrast to Virginians cooking Brunswick stew well before the start of the Civil War, according to an eyewitness account of Georgia barbecues in the early 1870s, we are told that "there was no Brunswick stew in those days." That testimony strongly implies that Brunswick stew wasn't a regular feature of barbecues in Georgia until at least the last two decades of the nineteenth century.[81]

By 1863, street vendors in Virginia were offering Brunswick stew for sale, and soldiers in Virginia enjoyed meals of real Brunswick stew in Virginia during the Civil War.[82] Some were also the victims of unscrupulous vendors from time to time. On one occasion during the Civil War, authorities arrested two vendors in Petersburg, Virginia, and whipped them with thirty lashes for trying to sell Brunswick stew to Confederate soldiers that they made with dog meat.[83]

It appears that Brunswick stew wasn't a popular stew in Georgia until after the Civil War ended. It is possible that Confederate soldiers returning home to Georgia after serving in Virginia carried the recipe back to Georgia with them after the end of the war. The recipe may have gained popularity in Georgia from letters, newspapers, traveling barbecue cooks or even a cookbook that has been lost to time. Another possible explanation for how Brunswick stew arrived in Georgia is through settlers who went there from Virginia. By the 1850s, there were so many Virginians living in and around Wilkes, Cass and Cherokee Counties that people called the region "Little Virginia."[84] Moreover, by the 1840s, Georgians were holding events that they called "old Virginia barbecues." Because "a Virginia barbecue would not be complete" without Brunswick stew, this is a very plausible explanation for how Brunswick stew was introduced in Georgia years before it became widely popular there.[85]

Even though Georgians have a lot of enthusiasm for Brunswick stew, the evidence they have for it originating in Georgia is inadequate for a convincing argument. Even the *New Georgia Encyclopedia* credits Brunswick, Virginia, as being the original home of Brunswick stew.[86] As Edwin T. Williams observed, "It is very evident that our Georgia friends were misled by the coincidence in names."[87]

Virginians are as vehement in their claim of being the inventors of Brunswick stew as are Georgians. In recent times, the controversy between the two states has been spirited. In 1999, Virginians and Georgians competed in a "stew off" in Lawrenceville, Virginia, to determine who made the best Brunswick stew. A Virginia team won the first-place trophy. A few days later, the trophy showed up in Brunswick, Georgia, on the mayor's desk. No one claimed to know how it got there. The Virginia team's stew master threatened, "If they don't send it back, we'll just go down there and win it again."[88]

Charlette Woolridge (*left*) serving up award-winning Virginia-style Brunswick stew in Richmond, Virginia, celebrating Brunswick Stew Day in 2017. *Author's collection.*

The legislatures in Georgia and Virginia both passed proclamations and resolutions declaring that their state is the rightful birthplace of Brunswick stew. In January 1988, the Virginia General Assembly attempted to put the debate to rest by issuing a proclamation citing Brunswick County, Virginia, as "the place of origin of this astonishing gastronomical miracle."[89] In 2002, the Virginia House of Delegates and Senate designated the fourth Wednesday of each January as Virginia's official Brunswick Stew Day. The team that wins first place at the annual "stew off" held in Alberta, Virginia, during the Taste of Brunswick Festival has the honor of cooking a huge iron kettle of Brunswick stew on Virginia's Capitol Square grounds in Richmond. The stew is served freely to all who get there within the short amount of time it takes to empty the ninety-gallon iron kettle.

A Virginia Tradition

Brunswick Stew Legend and Lore

Over the centuries, people have cooked up an entertaining collection of stew stories to explain the origin of Brunswick stew. James Cresap Sprigg Jr. bought the Smithfield Ham and Products Company Inc. in 1925 and remained active in running the business for several decades. He claimed that Brunswick stew originated in fifteenth-century England. According to Sprigg, what we call Brunswick stew was a "Mag" stew consumed in the summertime in order to, as he put it, "load up" on vegetables in an effort to prevent diseases like scurvy and beriberi. Because Sprigg's sales brochures for Brunswick stew claimed that his product was "[p]repared according to an old Virginia recipe dating back to colonial times," one must assume that he believed English colonists brought the recipe to Virginia in, according to the labels on the cans, "early colonial times."[90]

In 1916, avid hunter and Civil War veteran Horace Hilliard Heartwell, one of Brunswick's "oldest and most prominent citizens," claimed to be the inventor of Brunswick stew. At around the turn of the twentieth century, he directed the preparations for many barbecues held in that county. Before he died in 1916, Heartwell claimed that the first Brunswick stew was prepared at his home in Brunswick County, Virginia, with his help.[91] If he mentioned the actual date of that momentous achievement, no one recorded it.

In 1927, Mr. R.L. Justice shared an old account of the origin of Brunswick stew at a barbecue he hosted in Columbia, Tennessee, where he observed what the news reporter called "the old Virginia custom." According to Justice, long ago in Brunswick County, Virginia, an old Virginia colonel served the first Brunswick stew to his friends. To acquire the ingredients for the stew, the colonel went hunting early in the morning. He returned later in the morning with several squirrels and birds and gave them to his butler along with some vegetables that he picked from his garden. Unknown to the colonel, his butler had been drinking all morning and continued to do so throughout the day. Inebriated, his butler put all the meats and vegetables into a pot and left them to simmer all day long. Only discovering that his butler was intoxicated soon before his guests arrived, the colonel had no choice but to serve the stew to his guests for dinner. However, the colonel was pleasantly surprised at how delicious the stew was, and his guests also enjoyed it greatly. From that time forward, the colonel regularly served the stew to guests. At one dinner, the colonel asked his friends, "What should I call this delicious dish?" They all agreed that it should be named "Brunswick stew" to honor its county of origin.[92]

Perhaps the colonel referred to in the story above is a fellow known as Colonel Homes. Another account of Brunswick stew's origin that is similar to Mr. Justice's account tells how a prominent citizen of Brunswick County, Virginia, named Colonel Homes first cooked Brunswick stew after he and his hunting party returned from a successful squirrel hunt. Being hungry, the hunters raided a neighbor's garden for vegetables and cooked them in a large pot with the squirrels, and Brunswick stew was born.[93]

In 1901, stew master Augustine Royall of Powhatan County, Virginia, told his version of the first Brunswick stew. Sometime in the eighteenth century, according to Royall, some men from Powhatan County, Virginia, camped in Brunswick County during a hunting trip. They chose one member of the hunting party each day to perform cooking duty. One of the hunters was lazy, and on his appointed day to cook, he haphazardly threw random foods into a large pot, added salt, black pepper and red pepper and let it simmer. When the hunting party returned to camp that evening, they were angry that there was only one pot of food prepared. However, after tasting the stew, they all praised the lazy cook and demanded that he share the recipe. Someone suggested that the lazy chef name his one-pot meal "Brunswick stew" in honor of where it was first cooked. The others agreed, and Brunswick stew was born.[94]

In 1978, the Virginia Department of Agriculture and Consumer Services published a booklet claiming that people in Jamestown, Virginia, were the first to cook Brunswick stew. Colonists, they claimed, learned to cook it from the Powhatan Indians. The stew's ingredients included corn, beans and wild game that the Powhatan Indians simmered for hours in large earthen pots. How the dish came to be called Brunswick stew, the story goes, "is a mystery lost somewhere in the dusty archives of Colonial history." Of course, officials in Brunswick County were not happy. Brunswick County administrator Jesse L. Fowler bristled, "I am personally offended; the county should be offended." He formally expressed his displeasure in a strongly worded letter addressed to the agriculture commissioner, the department's director of information and the editor of the booklet.[95]

In support of the claim that Powhatan Indians in Jamestown, Virginia, cooked the first "Brunswick stew," some have offered old accounts of Governor Spotswood's visit to Fort Christianna in 1716. Located in what is today Brunswick County, Virginia, Governor Spotswood established the fort in order to provide Christian education and protection for friendly Native

A Virginia Tradition

Left: You know Brunswick stew is done when it is thick enough to hold the paddle up straight. *Author's collection*.

Right: Ladling the stew in Richmond, Virginia, on Brunswick Stew Day in 2017. *Author's collection*.

Americans who lived in the region. During Spotswood's 1716 visit to the fort, he dined on an "unnamed stew" provided by his Indian guests. When officials established the Brunswick County government in 1732, the people of Jamestown celebrated the event by reenacting Spotswood's visit to the fort. They hired an Indian family who lived near Jamestown to prepare a stew like the one enjoyed by the governor that was, supposedly, created from descriptions of it in records that were available at that time. Jamestown officials and several people who had lobbied for the creation of Brunswick County attended the feast. This Brunswick County "Indian-style" stew, proponents of this theory claim, was actually the first Brunswick stew in history. Although first cooked in Brunswick County, it received its name from the people of Jamestown.[96] Interestingly, some in Emporia, Virginia, claim Spotswood's Brunswick County Indian stew as the ancestor of their famous chicken muddle.

The local tradition in Brunswick County, Virginia, is probably the most well-known account of how Brunswick stew was born there. The county proudly displays its tradition on roadside historical markers all around Brunswick County, Virginia, for all to see.[97] With the headline "The Original Home of Brunswick Stew," the markers display the following account of the origin of Brunswick stew:

> *According to local tradition, while Dr. Creed Haskins and several friends were on a hunting trip in Brunswick County in 1828, his camp cook, Jimmy Matthews, hunted squirrels for a stew. Matthews simmered the squirrels with butter, onions, stale bread, and seasoning, thus creating the dish known as Brunswick stew. Recipes for Brunswick stew have changed over time as chicken has replaced squirrel and vegetables have been added, but the stew remains thick and rich. Other states have made similar claims but Virginia's is the first.*

Although claimed by Brunswick County's local tradition, there is no credible written record that hunters there first cooked Brunswick stew in 1828 during a hunting trip. In fact, the best records available indicate that the first Brunswick stew master cooked it there at least twelve years earlier.

The Birth of Brunswick Stew

In 1906, a newspaper printed an account of the first salvo in the twentieth century revival of the Great Brunswick Stew Controversy. According to the article, the originator of the delicious dish was one of two men who lived in antebellum Brunswick County, Virginia. The inventor of the stew was either a fellow named Mr. Haskins or a fellow named Mr. Stith. According to the article, both men claimed to have been the first to cook Brunswick stew. However, the author lamented, both of those men died before resolving the controversy.[98] Unknown to the author at that time, a well-documented account of the origin of Brunswick stew was about to be published.

In 1907, the Brunswick County, Virginia Board of Supervisors published letters written by people with firsthand knowledge of the stew's origin. The "Brunswick stew letters," as I call them, represent the most reliable accounts of the origin of Brunswick stew available. The letters also corroborate an older account of the origin of Brunswick stew published in a letter in 1886.

It is probable that the tomato is served and cooked in a greater variety of ways than any other article of diet known. Just here hangs a tale. It has long been a disputed point as to what was the origin of the Brunswick squirrel stew. Now, gentle reader, don't be startled when I say that the squirrel stew was made some sixteen years before the tomato was known in this country. During the War of 1812, between the United States and England, there was a man by the name of James Matthews who was a soldier in said war. He was from the Red Oak neighborhood in Brunswick county, VA.—It appears that he claimed his brother's house as his home, but being of a roving disposition and a man of refinement he was a most welcome visitor wherever he stopped, in fact made himself useful in doing little odd jobs in the household department, particularly in the kitchen. He was also a great squirrel hunter, and it was his way of cooking the squirrel which gained him such popularity and éclat among the ladies. His mode of cooking the squirrel was quite simple, as follows: After dressing it nicely, the squirrel was set to cooking early in the morning, so that it might be ready for a two o'clock dinner. It was kept stewing continually, water being added to supply evaporation, until it was thoroughly done that the flesh would separate from the bones, which were taken out and the stew seasoned to taste, not having any vegetable whatever in it. This was the first Brunswick stew, of 1816, and continued to be until 1830–32, when the tomato had become better known as a most excellent vegetable. About this time a man by the name of Ned Stith [from the same county] conceived the idea of improving "Matthew's stew" by the addition of the tomato, onion, corn, potatoes, middling, fresh butter and lightbread. I will now proceed to give the original recipe, after the tomato was known to bear so important a part in luxurious living: Take one squirrel fresh and nice, a half-pound of middling cut thin and with skin off, and water in sufficient quantity. Put on at 8 o'clock to cook for five hours, when the flesh will leave the bones of the squirrel, which should be taken out. Now add one quart of tomatoes (peeled), one small onion, one-half pound of butter (fresh) and one good size Irish potato, two ears of corn with the grains split down each row before cutting from the cob. Then a sufficient quantity of sweet lightbread should be added with the tomatoes just one hour before dinner. Now season to the taste with both black and red pepper and you have the genuine Brunswick squirrel stew. It is a remarkable fact that no other flesh will impart the delicate flavor as the squirrel, hence there is nothing whatever to take its place. It is true that a good stew can be made from fowls, veal or lamb; but I think that the best made (after squirrel) is from the common snapping turtle, which makes a most delicious dish, in imitation of the genuine stew. But an epicure will detect at once that the wild squirrel flavor is wanting and cannot be imparted by any other flesh.

Signed, Tar Heel

Macon Telegraph, "Brunswick Stew," August 19, 1886

In 1886, twenty-one years before the publication of the Brunswick stew letters, the *Macon Telegraph*, in Georgia of all places, printed a letter originally published in the *Petersburg Index-Appeal* signed with the pen name "Tar Heel." Tar Heel's account of how "Brunswick squirrel stew" was born in Brunswick County, Virginia, long before tomatoes became popular in the United States in the 1830s, is remarkably similar to the Brunswick stew letters' account. The Tar Heel letter focuses on a veteran of the War of 1812 who lived in Brunswick County, Virginia, named James Matthews. Matthews, the story goes, was a great squirrel hunter who first made his legendary squirrel stew in 1816. According to the article, Matthews started cooking early in the morning by simmering squirrels in a large pot of water. When the meat was at the right level of tenderness, he separated it from the bones, which he discarded. He then returned the meat to the pot. The stew was ready to eat by two o'clock in the afternoon. Matthews did not put vegetables of any kind in his stew.

Matthews's original recipe changed little until the early 1830s. Around that time, a fellow named Ned Stith, also of Brunswick County, decided to improve on "Matthews' stew" by adding tomatoes, corn, butterbeans and potatoes, thus giving us the classic Virginia-style Brunswick stew recipe.[99] This 1886 account of Brunswick stew's origin differs little from the account in the 1907 Brunswick stew letters. In addition to containing more details about James Matthews than the 1907 letters, the 1886 article mentions Ned Stith. Needham (Ned) Langhorne Washington Stith was born in Brunswick County, Virginia, in 1800. He married Lucy Gray Haskins on July 20, 1825. They had eight children. He is descended from the first clerk of Brunswick County, Colonial Drury Stith. He died in 1840.[100] Matthews turned squirrel soup into squirrel stew. Ned Stith put the finishing touches on the recipe by adding the vegetables, and Matthews's stew became Brunswick stew as we know it today.

The witnesses of so many credible, firsthand accounts of Brunswick stew's origin in Brunswick County, Virginia, make it clear that Brunswick stew is a genuine Virginian dish. The following paragraphs comprise a summary of the best accounts of the history of Brunswick stew.

When Governor Spotswood established Fort Christianna in 1716 in what is today Brunswick County, Virginia, it was an untouched wilderness on Virginia's western frontier. People used to say of Brunswick County in those days, "A squirrel could go from one end of the county to the other without ever touching the ground."[101] Fort Christianna attracted the first flood of English settlers to the region, and they immediately started clearing land

Chiles Cridlin of the Proclamation Stew Crew stirring a huge kettle of delicious, old-fashioned Virginia-style Brunswick stew. *Courtesy Chiles Cridlin.*

in order to establish plantations and farms. After farmers started growing crops, you can bet that squirrels were there to exploit the abundance of food surrounded by the safety of tall trees. In response, the farmers organized squirrel hunts to rid their fields of the pests. Naturally, people there became expert at preparing barbecued squirrels and squirrel soup. By 1732, the Brunswick County government had been established, complete with a courthouse and a prison.

In the early nineteenth century, a man named James ("Uncle Jimmy") Matthews lived at Mount Donum on the banks of the Nottoway River in Brunswick County, Virginia. Matthews was a veteran of the War of 1812. He was also an avid squirrel hunter. His skills were no doubt put to good use protecting local farms from the destructive little tree dwellers. His squirrel hunting skills, combined with the fact that he was a good cook, made him particularly suited for perfecting delicacies made with squirrel meat. Sometime around 1816, he improved the thin, colonial-era squirrel soup by transforming it into what would become his famous, hash-like squirrel stew. Unlike the watery squirrel soup people were accustomed to eating, Matthews's stew was rich and flavorful. Similar to hash recipes, Matthews's squirrel stew was cooked until the squirrel meat was very tender, it contained a generous amount of onions and was thickened with bread.

By 1828, Matthews was an "old man" and a "retainer" of a Virginia legislator named Dr. Creed Haskins (1796–1848). Haskins lived in what was called "the Grove" in Brunswick County.[102] Haskins's family goes back in Virginia to the year 1689, when Edward Haskins arrived from England to settle on the James River near Richmond, Virginia. Often, Haskins employed Matthews to cook for his guests and for public events that he hosted. Matthews simmered his delicious hash-like squirrel stew made with middling, onions, butter, stale bread, salt and pepper for several hours until the meat was tender and the broth thick. There were no vegetables in Matthews's original version of the stew; those who preferred vegetables ate them as side dishes. By 1828, Matthews was regularly cooking the stew at picnics and public gatherings, which gained Matthews a stellar reputation as a squirrel stew master.

After Matthews's death, Dr. Aaron Haskins, who occasionally added a little brandy or Madeira wine to his version, became the caretaker for the "original squirrel stew" recipe. His cousin Jack Stith was his successor. William Thomas Mason (1820–1897), called "Colonel Tom" in the letters, succeeded Jack Stith. By the 1830s, tomatoes were becoming a widely popular food in the United States. Although Jack Stith was the caretaker of the original recipe, it was in that decade that Ned Stith added the tomatoes, potatoes, corn and butterbeans to Matthews's squirrel stew and the "gastronomic miracle" was born.[103] Named after the Virginia County in which it was first cooked, Brunswick stew became a famous dish in Virginia and all over the world.

Dr. Creed Haskins and Ned Stith's association with the invention of Brunswick stew is consistent with the 1906 article about the first argument over who invented the dish. Both "Mr. Haskins" (Dr. Creed Haskins), who became the caretaker of Matthews's "original squirrel stew" recipe, and "Mr. Stith" (Needham Stith), who improved it by adding vegetables, played roles in transforming James Matthews's squirrel stew into Brunswick stew. However, Haskins was simply a caretaker of the recipe. The real credit for inventing the stew belongs to James Matthews for transforming squirrel soup into his delicious version of squirrel stew and Needham Stith for perfecting it by adding potatoes and the Virginia trinity.

In addition to the Tar Heel letter and the Brunswick stew letters, there is also the letter written to the editor of the *Richmond Times-Dispatch* in 1946 by Colonel William Thomas Mason's (mentioned in the Brunswick stew letters) daughter-in-law, Mrs. Bell K. Mason. Mrs. Mason was born in Brunswick County, Virginia, in 1865. In her letter, she recounted the many times she enjoyed Brunswick stew cooked under the supervision of "Colonel Tom" in the Grove at the home of Jim Haskins. She stated that Brunswick stew "originated with the Masons, Haskins, and Stiths of Brunswick" County, Virginia.[104]

From Matthews's Stew to Brunswick Stew

In addition to Brunswick County, Virginia, people who live in just about every other locality in the United States with a city, town or county named Brunswick have claimed their spot to be the stew's original home.[105] Brunswick stew enthusiasts who lived in places not named "Brunswick" explain that the stew didn't receive its name from a city or a county. Instead, people named it in honor of Caroline of Brunswick, wife of King George IV.[106] As mentioned earlier, others, specifically Texans and North Carolinians, simply changed the name of the stew in unsuccessful attempts to bring peace to the stew wars galaxy.[107]

According to the best records available, Jimmy Matthews's stew masterpiece was known simply as "squirrel stew" while Matthews was alive. It wasn't widely known as Brunswick stew until the 1840s. Two years before stew master Creed Haskins died in 1848, the stew was just beginning

> Meade Haskins, Blackstone, Virginia, to Dr. T. James Taylor, Cochran, Virginia, May 22, 1907
>
> My Dear Doctor,—In response to your request to tell you what I know of the origin of "Brunswick stew," I send you a copy of the receipt given me by my father, Dr. Richard Edward Haskins, in his life time for what was known to him as the original "Brunswick stew." It is labeled "Original Squirrel Stew, by Dr. A.B. Haskins, of Brunswick County, Va."
>
> This is it:
>
> "Parboil squirrels until they are stiff (half done), cut small slices of bacon (middling), one for each squirrel; one small onion to each squirrel (if large one to two squirrels), chopped up. Put in bacon and onions first to boil, while the squirrels are being cut up for the pot. Boil the above until half done, then put in butter to taste; then stale loaf bread, crumbled up. Cook this till it bubbles, then add pepper and salt to taste. Cook this until it bubbles and bubbles burst off. Time for stew to cook is four hours with steady heat."
>
> Note.—While cooking keep a tea kettle of hot, boiling water to add to pot as necessary. Vegetables are not in the original "Brunswick stew." Those who prefer vegetables add them after the stew is done, in their plates.
>
> I.E. Spatig, *Brunswick County, Virginia: Information for the Homeseeker and Investor*, 1907

to be widely known as Brunswick stew.[108] An account in an 1846 edition of the *Richmond Enquirer* described a squirrel stew with the note, "called by some a Brunswick Stew."[109] In 1853, the famous nineteenth-century Virginia barbecue cook Thomas Griffin used to advertise "stewed squirrel" on his menu along with Virginia-style barbecued pork and barbecued squirrels. When reminiscing about the "past glories of old Tom Griffin's incomparable concoctions" in 1881, a writer for the *Daily Dispatch* referred to Griffin's "stewed squirrel" as "Brunswick stew."[110] By 1849, Virginians were recognizing Brunswick stew as a "genuine South-side dish composed of squirrels, chickens, a little bacon, corn, and tomatoes, *ad libitum*," which was a nod to its southern Virginia roots in Brunswick County.[111]

There is no record that Matthews, Stith or Haskins were the first to name the stew after Brunswick County, Virginia. That honor goes to the people of Petersburg, Virginia. Dr. T. James Taylor of Cochran, Virginia, who wrote one of the Brunswick stew letters, described the process of how, sometime in the 1830s, the people of Petersburg, Virginia, started bragging on the delicious squirrel stew they enjoyed while visiting Brunswick County. Consequently, they were the first to give the stew the name "Brunswick stew."[112]

Brunswick Stew Masters

The appetizing aroma of a huge kettle of Virginia-style Brunswick stew simmering outside over an open fire is irresistible. On Brunswick Stew Day in 2017 at the Virginia State Capitol in Richmond, a young woman hurriedly approached the cook site where ninety gallons of old-fashioned Virginia-style Brunswick stew was slowly simmering. Out of breath, she explained, "I was four blocks away headed in the other direction when I was stopped in my tracks by the most wonderfully appetizing aroma. I had to follow my nose to find out what it was." She was from Minnesota, and this was her first encounter with what's been called Virginia's "sacred delicacy."[113] After one taste, she was thankful that she made the four-block walk to find the source of the enticing aroma.

Bill Steed and his son, Chad, of the Farm Life Stew Crew were the stew masters that day. Those two have Brunswick stew in their blood. Bill's family tree goes all the way back to Dr. Creed Haskins himself. Clearly, Bill loves what he is doing. He enthusiastically described to me the great effort required to cook a ninety-gallon pot of Brunswick stew. However, he does take advantage of at least one labor-saving tool. "I use a French fry cutter to chop the potatoes and onions. It saves me a lot of work," he explained with a friendly grin. It was ten o'clock in the morning, and he and his stew crew had been cooking since way before the sun came up. They work together like a finely tuned machine. One stirs with a long-handled paddle. Another cook searches for imperfections and points them out to a third cook, who reaches in with a small spatula to remove the offender, such as the lone kidney bean that somehow always makes its way into a package of butterbeans.

Bill and his stew crew earned the honor of cooking Brunswick stew in Richmond on Brunswick Stew Day by winning the prestigious annual

Stew master Bill Steed and his Farm Life Stew Crew cooked ninety gallons of award-winning Virginia-style Brunswick stew in Richmond, Virginia, on Brunswick Stew Day in 2017. Delegate Tommy Wright takes a turn at stirring the pot. *Left to right*: William Steed, Chad Steed, Zach Maitlad, Tommy Wright, Brenda Ruddick, Chuck Maitlad, Beverly Steed, Bill Steed and Deborah Steed. *Author's collection.*

"stew off" held in October 2016 at the Taste of Brunswick Festival. There is fierce competition every year, and only the very best stew comes out as the winner. Bill's stew is no exception. It is thick and rich with flavor imparted by the meats and the vegetables. There is no visible sign of onions or potatoes; they melt into his stew during the long cook. Bill doesn't share many of his stew secrets. When I started fishing for them, he reluctantly admitted, "I use a little beef with the chicken in my stew, but I can't tell you much more than that."

At about eleven o'clock in the morning, the grand kettle of toothsome Virginia-style Brunswick stew was ready to serve. Anyone who wanted his or her share of it had to get there early. Hungry Richmonders had emptied the ninety-gallon kettle of stew by two o'clock that afternoon.

Today, stew masters like Bill and Chad are preserving an old and cherished Virginia tradition. Most modern Virginian stew masters donate their time, energy and talent to cook gallons and gallons of stew every year for charities and other worthy causes. Their efforts pay tribute to the multitudes of pioneering Virginian stew masters who made Virginia's Brunswick stew legendary. Although history has forgotten the names of most of them, it couldn't erase the memory of them all or their legendary versions of delicious, old-fashioned, Virginia-style Brunswick stew. The following sections expound on that fact.

James Matthews

James Matthews, also known as Uncle Jimmy Matthews, was the first Brunswick stew master in history. He is famous for transforming Virginia's thin squirrel soup into rich, thick squirrel stew. Very little is known about him beyond scant mentions of him in official records and the limited information contained in the 1886 Tar Heel letter, which notes that he lived in the Red Oak district of Brunswick County, Virginia, and the 1907 Brunswick stew letters, which refer to him as "a retainer of Dr. Creed Haskins" and "an old man." In early nineteenth-century Virginia, the word *retainer* could refer to an employee or an enslaved African American body servant.[114]

A census taker recorded the name "James Matthews" in the federal census conducted in St. Andrews Parish in Brunswick County, Virginia, in 1820.[115] According to the census, James Matthews was a Caucasian who lived alone and was between twenty-six and forty-four years old. If the census taker accurately recorded his age, it seems to contradict the Brunswick stew letters, which describe him as an "old man" by 1828. At any rate, it appears that by 1840, James Matthews had either died or moved away from Brunswick County. The census taken twenty years later in 1840 doesn't list James Matthews's name, but it does list Samuel Matthews and Aaron B. Haskins. Virginia military records also list a James Matthews as having served in the War of 1812, which adds credibility to the 1886 Tar Heel letter that describes Matthews as a veteran of that war.[116] Matthews was a bachelor and "a man of refinement" with a "roving disposition." Those qualities, combined with his way of preparing squirrels in a stew, made him quite the ladies' man. The Tar Heel letter states that he enjoyed "popularity and éclat among the ladies."

Regardless of how famous James Matthews is for his legendary improvements to Virginia's squirrel soup, it is doubtful that he was the cook who chopped the onions and stirred the pots. In antebellum Virginia, most

> Dr. T. James Taylor, Cochran, Virginia, to Hon. I.E. Spatig, Lawrenceville, Virginia, June 3, 1907
>
> Dear Sir,—The "Brunswick stew," which is now made of all sorts of meat and all kinds of vegetables, was originally no such *olla podrida*. It was made of squirrels and onions principally, with plenty of butter, good Virginia middling and condiments. It was called simply "squirrel stew," but should have been called Haskin's stew or Matthews' stew, as it originated and was preserved by the former family, and its inventor James Matthews—glory to his memory. Like all good things its [Brunswick stew's] reputation extended to the neighboring counties and to the city of Petersburg, where it was known as "Brunswick stew" and so called. I have a personal knowledge of these facts, as I boarded when a school-boy in a family directly in the locality where this stew originated.
>
> I.E. Spatig, *Brunswick County, Virginia: Information for the Homeseeker and Investor*, 1907

cooks were African Americans—some of them free, most of them enslaved. In all likelihood, Matthews provided the recipe and supervised enslaved people who did the hard work of preparing the ingredients and cooking his squirrel stew.

Colonel Richard Thomas Walker Duke Sr.

Richard Thomas Walker Duke Sr. (1822–1898), also known as Walker Duke, was a nineteenth-century Congressional representative, Confederate veteran and lawyer who lived in Albemarle, Virginia. His son was Richard Thomas Walker Duke Jr., also known as Tom Duke. Walker Duke served his delicious Virginia-style Brunswick stew at barbecues hosted at his estate, named Sunnyside.[117] Duke's Brunswick stew was so delicious that one fellow offered $1,000 to anyone who could teach him to make "dat divine soup," which in today's dollars is well over the whopping sum of $15,000.[118] Tom Duke recorded many details of his father's old Virginia barbecues and Brunswick stew, complete with recipes. He wrote this account of his father's fish frys and stews in his *Recollections*:

A Virginia Tradition

An image from an older version of the label on James River Brand Smithfield Chicken Brunswick Stew depicting African American Brunswick stew cooks in Virginia. *Courtesy Isle of Wight County Museum. Used by permission.*

Father always wound up his excursion with a big fish fry & Brunswick Stew, to which he invited "the Hollow." He generally took along about five gallons of Monticello Claret, & brewed in a wash tub a claret punch which the Mountaineers called "Dog's blood." This was the only "spirituos [sic] refreshment" allowed & so these parties never became hilarious. Each Mountaineer brought a squirrel or so & failing a squirrel—a chicken & father prepared a big iron pot of his celebrated stew. Lest it be lost to a posterity hardly worthy of it, I give the receipt. In a large iron pot in which water was simmering over the fire were placed, corn & ochra [sic] & butter beans & tomatoes and a few potatoes—a generous piece of bacon—and the squirrels & chickens cut in small pieces, and a big lump of butter. To that was added a bottle of Worchester Sauce—large or small according to the size of the stew & the pot was allowed to boil slowly until the squirrels & chicken were "all to pieces." Just before the stew was ready to serve the trout were put in the frying pan & by the time the stew was eaten the fish was ready. Generally the Mountaineers brought chubs—which they had caught & there was an abundance to eat & drink, "topped off" with cups of black coffee.

Caesar Young and John Gilmore

Caesar Young and John Gilmore cooked barbecue and Brunswick stew at Tom Duke's events. Although Duke may have had a say in the famous Brunswick stew served at his barbecues, African American barbecue cooks supplied the true genius behind it. Until at least the early twentieth century, African Americans in Virginia were the most numerous and finest stew masters in the country. Regaling "their brother Knights with Old Dominion's famous Brunswick Stew" in Chicago in 1910, Freemasons there made sure to hire African American Brunswick stew cooks from Virginia to cook the stew.[119] Caesar Young and John Gilmore are two notable Virginian stew masters of that era.

Enslaved until the end of the Civil War, Caesar Young (1854–1935) and John Gilmore (1857–1937) often cooked Brunswick stew at public gatherings and Duke family barbecues.[120] Although Duke often got the credit, there is no doubt that Gilmore and Young's masterful stew skills

Left to right: Caesar Young, Judge R.T.W. Duke Jr., W.R. Duke and John Gilmore, circa 1900. *Courtesy Lucy D. Tonacci.*

made a delicious contribution to Duke's "barbecue stew." One author wrote of Gilmore and Young's Brunswick stew cooking skills: "John and Caesar hand the palm to 'Oscar' of the Waldorf on Hollandaise sauce but they will spot him cards and spades when it comes to Brunswick stew."[121]

Augustine Royall

At around the turn of the twentieth century, Augustine Royall (1849–1935), "Gus" to his friends, was called "the best authority in Virginia on Brunswick stew." Royall was born on his father's farm known as South Hill located on the James River in Powhatan County, Virginia. By 1933, Royall had been cooking Brunswick stew for seventy years.[122]

An unnamed woman who was enslaved by his family taught him how to cook Brunswick stew sometime before the start of the Civil War. Royall gave his recipe as follows:

> *Take two nice fat chickens or six squirrels and prepare them nicely and put them in a pot that will hold two and a half to three gallons of water; boil them until they are done enough for the bones to be easily gotten out; place the flesh on a dish or clean board and, with a sharp knife, chop it up fine and put it back in the water in which it has been boiled; to this add one-quarter of a pound of old bacon, chopped fine, two quarts of Irish potatoes, peeled and sliced thin, one quart of lima or butterbeans, split each bean and let them stand in a bucket of water for one-half hour; then rub them gently in your hands. This will cause the outer hull to leave the kernel and swim on top of the water and the kernel to sink. In this way you get rid of the tough indigestible skin; add two quarts of well-ripened, sound tomatoes; scald them and remove the skin; slice thin; add two large onions, sliced thin; add salt, red and black pepper to suite taste; one tablespoon of Worcestershire sauce. When all the ingredients are prepared and in, boil gently for five hours, and, as the water boils down, renew with hot water; stir constantly to keep from burning. When the stew is nearly done—or, say, been cooking four hours—put no more hot water in and have one dozen ears of green corn, shucked and all the silk removed, with a sharp knife split each row of grains on the cob; then shave off the tops of the grain with the knife; then, with the back of the knife-blade, press the corn so treated. The kernels will slip out of the husk, leaving that on the cob, and in this way you avoid the indigestible part of the corn. Put the corn in the pot or vessel*

one-half hour before taking the stew off the fire; add one-half pound nice fresh butter, and stir well, until thoroughly incorporated. The above will make enough to serve eight or ten persons. Serve hot (is very nice cold).[123]

As a teenager, Royall served in the Civil War. The Virginia Military Institute lists him as a member of the class of 1868. In 1864, he enlisted in Company C of the Virginia Military Cadets, eventually becoming a member of Company E, Fourth Virginia Cavalry. In 1896, he chaired the committee that helped erect a monument to his old company.

After the end of the Civil War, Augustine Royall became a successful businessperson in the Chesterfield, Virginia area. In 1872, he entered the real estate and insurance businesses. In 1879, he became a member of the town council. He was also an influential member of several clubs and associations, including the Powhatan Troop Association, the Free and Accepted Masons and the Independent Order of Odd Fellows.[124]

Royall's great fondness for Virginia's Brunswick stew shines in his description of it. Describing himself as "an admirer of the Brunswick stew," he went on to extoll the stew's virtues:

Brunswick stew, when properly made, is a royal dish, and has not only served to support "the inner man," but has made Presidents, Governors, Senators, legislators and all minor officers down to Justice of the Peace. Its influence in politics has been great indeed. It has also held a hand in card-playing and other kindred sports.

I am just here reminded of An Ode to Brunswick Stew written by the late lamented Dr. Leigh Burton, editor of the Baton. I can only recall a few lines, but sufficient to let you see he had not only true poetic fancy, but he had practical ideas about the dish and the surroundings to make it most enjoyable. Here is what he [wrote]: "Some shady nook, some sylvan spot; Some place to cook and hang the pot; Some place to drive our care away, Some place a little "draw to play."[125]

Royall admitted that his recipe for Brunswick stew was not the same as the one taught to him by his family's cook when he was a boy. He claimed, "I have greatly improved on the old methods of making it." His "improvements" included the addition of Worcestershire sauce and the unique practice of removing the outer husks from the beans and corn. It's hard to argue with success. According to those who enjoyed Royall's Brunswick stew, he knew a great deal about what he called the "subtle art" of making it.

A Virginia Tradition

John G. Saunders

John Goodrich Saunders (1868–1950), nicknamed "Dick" by his friends, was the city sergeant of Richmond, Virginia, in the 1920s.[126] By 1924, Saunders was recognized as "one of the best outdoor cooks in Virginia."[127] His delicious Brunswick stew sold for fifty cents a quart, and all proceeds always went to worthy causes.

Over the years, Sergeant Saunders raised thousands of dollars for charities, churches, the American Legion and other causes. He held one of his most famous stews in 1930 in order to raise funds for the widow of a police officer killed in the line of duty. He cooked six hundred gallons of stew that day. For six hours, Sergeant Saunders constantly stirred the simmering stew made with a recipe that he tailored to his own taste. He filled huge iron kettles with meats that included 780 pounds of chicken, 240 veal shins, 12 beef shins and 48 pounds of bacon. The vegetables included

City Sergeant Saunders of Richmond, Virginia, and his simmering Brunswick stew pot. *Courtesy Norman Rainock.*

800 pounds of potatoes, 360 pounds of cabbage, eighteen bushels of celery, seventy-two gallons of corn and 150 gallons of canned tomatoes, topped off with 48 pounds of butter. He perfectly seasoned the stew with salt, pepper and thyme. He auctioned off the last quart of stew from that day's cook for a whopping $10, which is the equivalent of $140 today.[128]

Although some declared that Saunders's stew was heretical because of the cabbage and celery, which are not traditional in Virginia-style stew, others raved that it was delicious.[129] In 1925, stew master Augustine Royall dined on Saunders's Brunswick stew and agreed with others that it was among the best they had ever eaten.[130]

Mary S. Sturdivant

Mary Sturdivant. From *12 Pearls*, 1924. *Author's collection.*

Mary S. Sturdivant (1832–1908) was born in Brunswick County, Virginia, to George White and his wife, Ann Elizabeth Mason. Her uncle on her mother's side was none other than William Thomas Mason (Colonel Tom), who appears in the Brunswick stew letters as a caretaker of the original Brunswick stew recipe. Mary married Edward Claiborne Sturdivant (1823–1919) in 1853. Eventually, she and her husband moved to the area around Brownsville, Tennessee, and she became famous there for her Virginia-style Brunswick stew, cooked using the recipe she brought with her from Brunswick, Virginia. Her son, Franklin Sturdivant (1860–1932), started a canning and packaging company in 1918. One of the products the company offered was Sturdivant's Old Virginia–Style Brunswick Stew. Around 1940, the family sold the packing company. In our times, her descendants are famous Brunswick stew cooks in Tennessee.[131]

Although Mary Sturdivant was the keeper of the recipe, she wasn't the person who did all of the work cooking Brunswick stew. A pamphlet titled *12 Pearls*, published by her son in 1924 to promote his mother's delicious

Left: Sturdivant Brand Old Virginia–Style Brunswick stew, circa 1920. *Author's collection.*

Below: Mrs. Sturdivant (Miss May) supervising the making of Brunswick stew. *Author's collection.*

Virginia-style Brunswick stew, depicts the way in which enslaved cooks toiled for hours, under the supervision of "Miss May," as they called Mrs. Sturdivant, doing the hard work required to cook large kettles of Brunswick stew. The Sturdivants weren't the first to offer canned Brunswick stew. Advertisements for Stockdell's "Genuine Georgia" Brunswick stew showed up in newspapers by 1899.[132]

Lillie P. Fearnow

Mrs. Fearnow's famous Brunswick stew is still available in stores today. *Courtesy Boone Brands.*

In the early 1920s, Lillie Pearl Fearnow (1881–1970) of Hanover County, Virginia, sold her first jar of homemade Brunswick stew. She took six pints of the stew to the Woman's Exchange in Richmond, Virginia, and quickly sold out. Soon, the mother of five was enlisting the help of two other women and their kitchens in order to cook enough of her delectably concocted Virginia-style Brunswick stew to meet the demands of customers. In 1946, she built a cannery, and by the time she first learned to drive a car after her sixty-seventh birthday in 1949, her Brunswick stew was a staple in pantries all over Virginia, North Carolina and beyond. According to Mrs. Fearnow, the secret to a good Brunswick stew is in the seasonings. That's why she personally seasoned all the Brunswick stew that came out of her factory until she died in 1970.[133] Mrs. Fearnow's delicious Brunswick stew is still available in stores today.

Anne Stone Davis

I met stew master Anne Stone Davis, "Stoney," also known as Anne Davis Kellum (1964–2016), at a stew I attended in Mechanicsville, Virginia, in 2014. She was overseeing the preparation of a sixty-five-gallon kettle of Virginia-style Brunswick stew. Anne learned to cook Brunswick stew from her father, Andrew Jack Davis (aka Daddy Jack). He was a famous stew master who cooked Brunswick stew for friends, churches and other community groups. He learned to cook the stew from his father, who learned it from his father. Daddy Jack passed the family's generations-old art of expertly cooking large kettles of old-fashioned Brunswick stew on to Anne. When he passed away, Anne inherited one of his old stew kettles and his cherished homemade stew paddles.

Anne was very particular about the quality of her stew. She had no tolerance for anything but perfection. She meticulously monitored the simmering stew, ensuring that everything about it was just right. On one rare occasion, when the stew didn't meet her high standards, she refused to serve it and tossed every ounce of it away.

Anne took the time to instruct me on the finer points of properly stirring a large kettle of Brunswick stew, which is a lot of hard work. Constant stirring is vital to prevent scorching, and stirring ninety gallons of stew with a wooden paddle can be as strenuous as shoveling snow. Therefore, proper technique is important, and Anne never hesitated to take the paddle away from anyone who wasn't stirring the stew properly.

Stew master Anne Stone Davis (aka Anne Davis Kellum) with Virginia congressman Dave Brat at a political stew at Mechanicsville, Virginia, in 2014. *Author's collection*.

> The secret of a good Brunswick stew is long, slow boiling. It should be started early in the morning and allowed to boil for several hours. Take 2 good-size squirrels, 3 quarts of cold water, 1 onion, and a strip of bacon—not pork [meaning don't use fatback]—and put them on to boil. It should boil 4 hours, unless the squirrel is very old and tough, in which case boil longer. When the meat has left the bones, remove the pot and pick out every piece of bone and skin, leaving the meat in shreds. Add to this stock 6 ears of corn cut from the cob, 1 quart of ripe tomatoes, 1-quart butter beans, 4 large Irish potatoes, and the juice of 1 lemon. Let this cook for another hour, stirring well to keep from burning. It should now be thick enough to eat with a fork, and is ready to serve. Add 1 tablespoon of Worcestershire sauce before serving.
>
> Carrie Picket Moore, *The Way to the Heart*, 1905

According to Anne's expert advice, first you need the right kind of paddle. It should be five feet long and homemade from ash or hickory wood. After the paddle, the proper stirring motion is paramount. Stand next to the kettle, facing the stew. Place the paddle blade flat against the top inside lip of the kettle closest to you and push down. Make sure the paddle blade remains in contact with the inside wall. It's as if you are scrapping the stew off the inside surface of the pot. Continue in a single motion all the way down to the bottom of the kettle and up the other side. Take a step to your left and repeat until you have circled the pot. Repeat continuously until the stew has finished cooking.

In 2016, Anne passed away far too soon at the age of fifty-two. In her lifetime, she celebrated her family's Brunswick stew tradition by cooking thousands of gallons of Virginia's "sacred delicacy" to support charities and other good causes. People who had the pleasure of enjoying a bowl of Anne's old-fashioned Brunswick stew with friends and family fondly remember the occasions with happy smiles and warm hearts. If that's a measure of a stew master's skill, and it is, Anne was one of the greatest.

Chapter 6
BURGOO

With the coming of the county fair and the opening of the fall campaign, there come also the days when the burgoo kettle sings and men, large of girth and of gustatory appreciation, gather for the feast. There are many friends of the burgoo offering who proudly claim it is in a class by itself.

Originally a native product of Kentucky burgoo is still most popular and most in evidence in that state, but migratory Kentuckians have carried its secrets to many parts of the country. Wherever it has been prepared by one versed in the secrets of its component parts and methodical preparation it has been a welcome friend and has claimed a large following.

Burgoo is food and drink, if one considers its varied ingredients. It has the materials for soup, it has vegetables, grains and meats, each in proper proportion, each introduced into the huge kettle at the proper time and in regular sequence, the final offering being a steaming hot, highly seasoned soup filled with cooked meats.

It has a flavor that no one has even adequately described, an appeal to the man of vigorous appetite which he has no desire to resist, a satisfying quality that would mean universal disarmament if all the potentates of earth could be gathered around the steaming cauldron as the offering is served.

Kentucky has been famous for many products sent forth to the world. Among these, not so widely known, but popular wherever known, is the offering of burgoo. Long may the burgoo kettle sing.
—Plain Dealer, *"Burgoo," August 23, 1914*

In 1896, the *New York Journal* reported that burgoo "is a stew of local fame and made up of everything a Kentuckian can get his hands on. It takes the place of an entire bill of fare, and few tables can boast of greater variety than can the composition of burgoo."[1] A Tennessee newspaper called it "Kentucky Brunswick stew" in 1890.[2] In 1902, a writer for the *Newark Advocate* wrote, "Burgoo is a distinctly Kentucky institution that is concocted and dispensed with Kentucky liberality."[3] In 1914, an anonymous writer told of the meats, grains and vegetables in "proper proportions" that are introduced to huge kettles of burgoo at the proper time and sequence. The final product, the author concludes, is a delightful, steaming-hot, highly seasoned dish that can be enjoyed "free from the dread of indigestion while laughing to scorn the pain of gout."[4] I'm not sure if that's an endorsement or not. A dictionary published in 1914 describes burgoo as "a kind of soup made with many different kinds of meat and vegetables, highly peppered and served very hot: popular in Kentucky and other places, especially at barbecues, picnics, and other outdoor feasts."[5] The writer of an article about "Burgoo Day" held in Shelbyville, Illinois, in 1916 described burgoo as "a boiled concoction of chicken, beef, corn, tomatoes—a sort of southern states chili."[6]

J.A. Estes wrote of burgoo in 1930, "You can serve a feast with a bowl and a spoon."[7] Moreover, although there might be reluctant agreement among many that burgoo is both "food and a drink," some describe it as more of a "soupy stew," while others vehemently disagree and hold that it is a "stewy soup."[8] Kentucky-born Missouri senator George Graham Vest (1830–1904) described burgoo by comparing it to the soup that Meg Merrilies served to Dominie Sampson in Sir Walter Scott's *Guy Mannering*.[9] A similar claim was made in 1855 for Brunswick stew.[10] Kentucky-born author and humorist Irvin S. Cobb described burgoo this way in 1917:

> *Do you know burgoo? If not your education has been sadly neglected—most woefully neglected. It is a glorified gumbo, made in copper caldrons over open fires; and it contains red meats and white meats, and ducks and chickens, and young squirrels and squabs, and all the fresh green vegetables in season. And into it with prodigal black hands the cooks put plenty of tomatoes for color and potatoes for seasoning and onions for flavour* [sic]. *And all these having stewed together for hours and hours, they merge anon into a harmonious and fragrant whole. So now the product is dipped up in ladles and bestowed upon the assemblage in tin cups, to be drunk after a fashion said to have been approved by Old Hickory Jackson Himself.*[11]

A Virginia Tradition

Burgoo shares the same squirrel soup ancestor as Brunswick stew. That is one reason why both of those stews are associated with social gatherings and barbecues. However, unlike Brunswick stew, burgoo never really became a famous dish all over the South. As a result, many who are not from Kentucky are not acquainted with the stew, which has resulted in some humorous stories over the years. A Kansas newspaper asked in 1885, "There are too many political terms being invented—what is 'burgoo'?"[12] In 1892, while a group of Philadelphians was visiting Louisville, Kentucky, their host invited them to a burgoo to take place later that week. They cheerfully accepted the invitation even though they had no idea what a burgoo was. Later that night, while they were sleeping, a neighbor's peacock unleashed a disturbingly loud, ear-piercing call. Awakened by the startling noise, one of the Philadelphians blurted out, "That must be that burgoo!"[13]

The confusion over what is and isn't burgoo exists partly because there is no widely accepted recipe for burgoo as there is with Virginia-style Brunswick stew. Recipes for burgoo vary, but most call for a multitude of vegetables and meats; all burgoo masters make their own special version of it. The multitude of variations in burgoo recipes explains why the author of an article in a 1932 edition of the *San Antonio Light* declared, "It takes a magician to find out what's in it."[14] When asked, "What is burgoo?" in

Hearty burgoo made with beef and vegetables. *Author's collection.*

1878, Illinois senator Luther Dearborn answered, "It's where they put an ox into a kettle of hot water, and boil him up, horns, hide, hoofs and all."[15] Senator Vest answered the question by saying, "My dear sir, the man doesn't live who can tell you what burgoo is for the simple reason that no two kettles of burgoo were ever made alike."[16] He explained that burgoo is prepared with care and skill by experts who claim to have some secret process in its preparation unknown to the uninitiated. Events called "burgoos," Vest recounted, were usually located near some famous spring, and the best time for such an event is in the middle or latter part of August or September, when vegetables are abundant, especially young corn, tomatoes and potatoes. Farmers also supplied chickens, squirrels, apples, watermelons and cider for the festivities.[17]

In 1888, a newspaper columnist wrote about the variable nature of burgoo recipes, "Burgoo is a noble, strengthening, out-of-door soup made on the go-as-you-please plan. What is put in it varies by the season, and the skill of the maker counts for no little."[18] Marion Harland also noticed the "never-the-same" characteristic of burgoo.[19] Writing for the *Evening Public Ledger*, Harland responded to a reader who shared a burgoo recipe in 1916. She commented, "The inquiry concerning the composition of the dish with the ungainly name has brought to our desk so many formulas, no two of which are alike, that we are both pleased and diverted. You contribute still another that varies from all its predecessors."[20]

The "go-as-you-please" nature of burgoo is hard to miss in an account of a burgoo attended by Senator Vest and his father near Frankfort, Kentucky, when he was a youngster. There was an immense kettle placed over a fire at the foot of a large sycamore tree. A celebrated African American burgoo cook named Uncle Larkin, adorned in his white apron, stirred the burgoo with a long-handled spoon. Vest recounted how he and several other hungry boys watched Uncle Larkin as he and his assistants prepared the stew. At just about the time that the stew was ready, a breeze overturned a jaybird's nest that was in the upper branches of the sycamore tree. Three poor little baby jaybirds dropped right into the kettle of stew. The spectators erupted in an expression of horror. They knew the stew was ruined! Nevertheless, Uncle Larkin didn't flinch. With a smooth, twisting motion of his long spoon, he submerged the birds into the stew and calmly explained, "Just in time, gentlemen; just in time."[21] This kind of thing probably gave rise to the tongue-in-cheek claim that burgoo is best cooked outdoors when June bugs and yellow flies are swarming.[22] Stew stories like that shed new light on the Bible verse, "I was a stranger, and ye took me in."

> 1898 Burgoo Recipe
>
> Put some red pepper in the bottom of a large iron cauldron, with potatoes, tomatoes, and corn; then put in half-a-dozen prairie chickens, as many more tender "yellow-legs" [barnyard chickens], and two dozen soft-shelled crabs; also some young squirrels if you can get any. Moisten with water until the solid contents begin to float; then hang the pot over the fire, and let the contents simmer for six hours, stirring continuously with a hickory stick. The hickory stick is believed to be the best, although there seems to be no valid reason why it should be selected in preference to any other. About an hour before it will be ready to serve, season with salt to taste; and when the meats are falling off the bones, the Burgoo is done.
>
> *The Encyclopedia of Practical Cookery*, 1898

Some claim that burgoo consists of any mixture of meats and vegetables cooked together in a soup or stew. That's an exaggeration. There are guidelines (as in "you should") and rules (as in "you must") for making burgoo; however, all of them are open to interpretation. A true burgoo must be thicker like a stew rather than thin like a soup. That's a rule. Certain vegetables are required such as potatoes, onions and tomatoes. J.M. Benton of Lexington, Kentucky, recounted the "spring wagon loads" of tomatoes being brought in for a burgoo catered by the nineteenth-century burgoo king Gus Jaubert. He wrote, "Next to the necessary quantity of meat, tomatoes constitute the chief ingredient in burgoo."[23] However, that's a guideline. After tomatoes, cooks can add just about any seasonal vegetable. That's a hard-and-fast burgoo rule.

Next, we come to the strict burgoo rule regarding acceptable proteins. Burgoo must contain at least one or a combination of the following, including but not limited to beef, pork, chicken, mutton, squirrel, rabbit, possum, raccoon, turtle, turkey, duck, goose, dove, squab, deer, buffalo, elk, moose, antelope, goat, lamb, pheasant, quail, groundhog, jackalope (if you can get it), grouse, woodchuck, beaver, oysters, mussels, squid or sturgeon (and so on). However, that list isn't exhaustive. When it comes to seasonings, the stew must contain the appropriate amounts of salt, black pepper and red pepper. That's a rule. Other spices and herbs can vary according to the cook's taste. That's a guideline. Some use spirits as a seasoning; others don't. It's not traditional to use leftover barbecued or roasted meats in burgoo as it is with hash. That's a guideline. Another important burgoo characteristic includes the long cooking time that allows the ingredients to soften and melt into the stew. That's a rule. Finally, the finished burgoo should be light brown to a reddish brown to a deep mahogany or any other appetizing color. Again, that's a guideline. Above all, the most important rule demands that every pot of burgoo must be unique. However, as a general guideline, that rule is also subject to interpretation. The most important burgoo rule to observe is this: all burgoo rules are made to be broken.

Some people incorrectly cook what they call "Brunswick stew" using just about any ingredient they have on hand. That's fine when cooking burgoo, but not Brunswick stew. This burgoo-like way of cooking Brunswick stew might explain why newspapers, magazines and other periodicals have occasionally published collections of unrelated general interest articles under the heading "Brunswick stew."[24]

Burgoo cooking rules are often more about what you shouldn't put into burgoo than what you should put into it. While some burgoo masters will freely tell you what they put in their burgoo, most are more eager to tell you what's *not* in it if you deviate from the "rules." After Marion Flexner, author of *Out of Kentucky Kitchens*, published a recipe for burgoo that included cabbage as an ingredient, the Kentucky-born poet, journalist and burgoo master James Tandy Ellis (1868–1942) expressed his strong displeasure. Ellis boasted that he had learned from the legendary burgoo king Gus Jaubert himself. Being appalled at the use of cabbage, he willingly shared his burgoo recipe with Flexner in order to correct her "error." His recipe calls for beef shank, chicken, lamb, potatoes, corn, garlic, butterbeans, tomatoes, onions, carrots, okra and green peppers seasoned with salt, black pepper and cayenne…but no cabbage.[25]

The "Ungainly Name"

Some have postulated that the word *burgoo* is a mispronunciation of the phrase "bird stew." Another theory holds that *burgoo* is the old Kentucky way of pronouncing the word *barbecue*.[26] Some have even claimed that *burgoo* is a Native American word for stew.[27] However, it appears that the word *burgoo* derives from the Turkish word for wheat porridge, which is *burghul*.[28] People in both Europe and the United States have called boiled oatmeal "burgoo" for centuries. Eliza Leslie included a recipe for burgoo in her 1837 cookbook

A Virginia Tradition

Tending the burgoo pots at a Kentucky barbecue in 1940. *Courtesy Library of Congress [LC-DIG-fsa-8a42935].*

that is simply a recipe for oatmeal mush.[29] Claude Choules was the last living male veteran of World War I. Before he died in 2011, he told of the oatmeal porridge called "burgoo" served by his grandmother when he was a child in Britain during the early years of the twentieth century.[30]

The oldest use of the word *burgoo* in English literature refers to a dish served to sailors in European navies at least as long ago as the 1650s.[31] The nautical version of burgoo (or *bargou*) consists of boiled oatmeal mixed with butter and, occasionally, molasses.[32] Some claimed that the "glorious victories" of the British navy wouldn't have been possible without the nautical stew's nourishing powers.[33] British sailors didn't share that belief. Referring to it sometimes as "loblolly" or "skillagallee," they complained that the bland seafaring burgoo never had enough butter in it.[34] The British navy served the nautical version of burgoo to American prisoners of war confined on British prison ships during the Revolutionary War. The Americans described it as being made of moldy oats boiled in large copper pots served to them in large tubs much like a farmer feeds his hogs.[35] The Royal Navy stopped serving burgoo onboard ships in 1797.[36]

There is also an old dish known specifically as "Scotch burgoo." An old English poem rhymes:

> *In my time I have swallowed much worse than this—*
> *And to give the candle-cup its due,*
> *'Tis almost as good as a Scotch burgoo.*[37]

Scotch burgoo was popular among the Scotch peasantry during the eighteenth and early nineteenth centuries. A recipe for Scotch burgoo published in 1823 described it as being much like hasty pudding made with boiled oats, salt and butter just like nautical burgoo.[38] Scottish historical records frequently mention oatmeal and porridge, which were main articles of food in Scotland centuries ago. Some recipes included meat, leeks, onions and other vegetables in addition to the oats.[39]

The word *burgoo* was in use during colonial and Federal times in Appalachia. People who settled near a tributary of the Elk River in and around the Randolph County, Virginia region, which became a part of West Virginia in 1863, started calling that tributary "Burgoo Creek" as far back as the last quarter of the eighteenth century.[40] People in Kentucky have referred to squirrel soup festivals as "burgoos" as far back as at least the 1830s. Chapman Coleman, the daughter of the famous Kentucky politician John J. Crittenden (1787–1863), wrote about the time American politician Daniel Webster (1782–1852) visited Crittenden in Frankfort, Kentucky, in 1836 and attended a "bergoo":

> *I cannot explain the origin of the word "bergoo"; the feast differed from a "barbecue," in that it was more primitive. Immense iron pots were kept on hand in some secluded spot, ready for such occasions, and each man was expected to bring his own tin cup and pewter spoon. "Bergoos" were always the order of the day when summer vegetables abounded; only one dish was prepared, but it was savory as the mess brought by Esau to his father, the blind patriarch. All the birds and squirrels round about were shot, prepared, and thrown indiscriminately into the large pots; then all the farms and gardens in the neighborhood were put under contribution, and young corn, tomatoes, peas, beans,—in short, every vegetable that could be found, was added. All this boiled away vigorously till the salutations of the day were over, family news told, and kindly questions asked and answered. The business of the day (which was making speeches and listening to them) concluded, then all present gathered around the steaming pots, cup and spoon in hand, to receive their portion.*[41]

Although no one knows for sure how or why the word *burgoo* came to be the name of Kentucky's famous stew, there are several inventive theories. Young E. Allison, a writer for the *Insurance Field*, jokingly explained in 1902 that the word is of Latin derivation—"burgus" meaning fortified and "googoo" meaning "very good" together gives us the word *burgoo*, which means "something very good that's fortified with other good things," where "good things" included the bourbon found in some versions of the stew.[42] In 1904, a fellow named Amos Kieth stumbled into the wrong Cincinnati hotel room and fell asleep after a night of carousing. Of course, the room's rightful guests were alarmed after they discovered the unconscious stranger. His defense presented to the police was that he had eaten too much burgoo.[43] In spite of these stew stories, the use of alcoholic beverages as ingredients in burgoo is not universal. The famous burgoo king Gus Jaubert claimed that he didn't use it in his recipe.[44] However, many others did.

An Indiana newspaper highlighted the association between burgoo and bourbon in 1887, stating, "Burgoo is a Kentucky barbecue soup. How nearly it is related to bourbon is not exactly known on this side of the river."[45] Some have claimed that the word *burgoo* is a combination of the words *bourbon* and *ragout*. This theory holds that people first called the stew "bourbon ragout" because some versions of it had bourbon in them. People eventually shortened the phrase to *bourbon goo* and, finally, transformed it into the word *burgoo*.[46] It appears that this theory is more about explaining the use of bourbon in burgoo recipes than it is about explaining the origin of the stew's name. However, the use of adult beverages in burgoo recipes did inspire its nicknames such as "burgood" and "beergood."[47]

Interesting theories aside, it may have been a custom of some Kentuckians in the eighteenth century to call any stew "burgoo." This seems to be the case in Robert J. Hearne's letter to the editor of *The Sun*, in which he wrote in 1909 about the "heavenly burgoo called Irish stew." On the other hand, perhaps the author was just waxing poetic.[48]

Another possibility to explain the Kentucky use of the word *burgoo* lies in the customs of Scotch-Irish settlers in western Virginia and Kentucky. They may have been the first to give the soup served at soup festivals the name "burgoo." As Scotch-Irish settlers moved into Kentucky in the eighteenth century, they may have looked on squirrel soup as an American version of Scotch burgoo that included corn instead of oatmeal. It was common for settlers and backwoods farmers to substitute corn for European grains such as wheat and oats, and this could explain the origin of using the word *burgoo* to describe squirrel soup.[49] The unique burgoo recipe with the

Slow-cooked burgoo made with beef brisket and garnished with peas. *Author's collection.*

"ungainly name" mentioned by Marion Harland in 1916 illustrates how settlers substituted corn for European grains. That old burgoo recipe calls for boiling duck, squirrel or chicken in a pot seasoned with salt and pepper until the meat is tender enough to pull from the bones. After pulling the meat and discarding the bones, the cook must stir the stew until the meat is "well shredded" before adding cornmeal to thicken the stew while it simmers for another thirty minutes. This burgoo is so thick when cooled it can be cut into slices. It seems very likely that this burgoo is an American adaptation of the old European Scotch burgoo. Instead of thickening the burgoo with oats, pioneers used the most readily available American grain, which was corn.[50] Therefore, it is a strong possibility that burgoo received its name from Scotch-Irish settlers.

Besides being the name of a stew, burgoo is also the name given to gatherings where the stew is the star attraction.[51] In the 1800s, a writer for the *New York Times* wrote that a burgoo event was an all-day picnic in the woods that puts New England's clambakes and Virginia's barbecues into the "deep shade of obscurity." In fact, at a burgoo, barbecue is just "a sort of incident."[52] No wonder political campaigners in Kentucky used to appoint an executive committee that they called the "Burgoo Committee," for the sole purpose of overseeing burgoo events.[53] Businesspeople in Owensboro,

Kentucky, established a burgoo club in the late nineteenth century. An account of the club from 1887 tells of not only the burgoo but also the festive nature of burgoo events, complete with speeches, dancing and a big pot of delicious burgoo washed down with copious amounts of adult beverages:

> *One of the features of Owensboro life is a burgoo club of about seventy-five members, consisting of the leading businessmen of the place. This club gives a burgoo (which, by way of explanation, is a barbecue, where birds, chickens, squirrels, beef, pork and dog, if one is handy, are thrown into an immense pot, stewed together, seasoned and eaten between drinks) every two weeks during the summer, and the fun these meetings afford keeps the boys laughing for the balance of twelve months. When attending a burgoo you are first asked to drink, and if you decline, you are made to drink. This drink is big enough to put you in fine shape, and you must then ascend a platform and dance before the crowd. It's no use to ask a man who has attended one of these burgoos if he danced, because he simply has to dance. Before the day is over every man is called upon for a speech, and a speech he is bound to deliver. It makes no difference how old a man is nor what position in society he holds; if he attends an Owensboro burgoo he must walk the chalk line and do as he is bid. The record for the past summer shows that Fred Clarke of the Sour Mash Distilling Company received several prizes as the best dancer on the grounds, while M.P. Mattingly got the prize for oratory.*[54]

Burgoo Legend and Lore

According to legend, long ago a Kentucky farmer hosted a hunting trip for his friends. After a long morning of hunting, the host asked his guests what they would like for dinner. The Mississippian wanted gumbo. The Virginian wanted sugar cured ham. The friend from Tennessee wanted hickory smoked ham. The Marylander wanted oysters. His friend from Arkansas wanted roast ham, and his Georgian friend wanted hog jowl. The Louisianan wanted duck. His friend from North Carolina wanted dumplings and squirrels. Frustrated, the Kentucky farmer exclaimed, "Aw, mix 'em all up and call it burgoo."[55]

Superstitious burgoo masters used to claim that to make a proper burgoo you must observe certain rituals and employ proper tools. For example, to ensure the best flavor, you must stir burgoo with a hickory stick.[56] In addition, the ideal burgoo must contain three geese that are neither borrowed nor begged. They must be stolen under the cover of darkness.[57] This holdover from the Virginia soup festivals ties the burgoo tradition to the Virginia soup tradition of contributing stolen chickens for the soup pot.

Although rabbit meat isn't a requirement for making burgoo, some believed that a rabbit's foot was a necessity. Informing readers of what a "burgoo" is in 1902, a writer for *The Standard* explained, "Burgoo is literally a soup composed of many vegetables and meats delectably fused together in an enormous cauldron, over which at the exact moment a rabbit's foot at the end of a blue yarn string is properly waved by a colored preacher whose salary has been paid to date."[58] Another version of the superstition states that the rabbit's foot must come from the rear left leg of "a graveyard rabbit, killed in the dark of the moon."[59]

As far back as the early nineteenth century, hosts expected every person attending a burgoo to bring a tin cup and spoon in order to partake of the feast.[60] This practice can be illustrated with a notice for a barbecue held in Scott County, Kentucky, displayed in a blacksmith's shop in 1843. The bill of fare included barbecued pigs, lambs, muttons and three hundred gallons of "first rate burgoo." The notice stated, "It will be expected that every gentleman who expects to eat Burgoo, will bring his cup and spoon."[61] The practice of requiring guests to bring their own cup and spoon began from necessity. Metal spoons and cups were scarce in remote areas, and it would have been difficult for a host to provide them for a large number of guests. By the late nineteenth century, the practice changed from guests bringing their own tin cup to hosts serving burgoo in tin cups. The famous burgoo king Gus Jaubert used to serve his burgoo to guests in tin cups and so did others. To meet the needs of a burgoo and barbecue held in Lexington, Kentucky, in 1912, the organizers ordered 28,800 pint-sized tin cups in which they served burgoo.[62]

Artists have captured burgoo's glory in poetry and song from time to time. In 1896, African Americans in Louisville performed a "burgoo song," written by Will S. Hayes (1837–1907), who was a famous poet, songwriter and boyhood friend of Gus Jaubert.[63] In 1895, Edward B. Jones expressed his admiration for the dish in a poem:

> *Shades of Sam Ward, whose gastric inspiration*
> *Made bouillabaisse, a blessing for the few;*
> *What would have been Kentucky's delectation*

A Virginia Tradition

If he had turned his talents to burgoo?
Beef, mutton, sassafras, tomato,
Peppers and okra, corn and onions new;
All these you'll taste, with peas and sweet potato,
*In that vast kettle of supreme burgoo.*⁶⁴

Another poet wrote:

Some certain things upon our mind
Did this impression make;
That Lexington's a bully town
*And "burgoo" takes the cake.*⁶⁵

By the nineteenth century, burgoo had gained a reputation for having mystical powers over voters. There was an old claim that "if you invite a Kentuckian to partake of a bourgoo [*sic*] at an open air picnic, you can make

"A Burgoo Feast," by Walter Edmunds. From *Frank Leslie's Illustrated Newspaper*, October 6, 1888. *Courtesy Western Kentucky University.*

him vote any ticket you want."⁶⁶ Many politicians took that belief to heart. In August 1898, it was reported that "burgoos are the means by which most of the crowds are gathered in the mountain districts [of Kentucky], and several of these political gatherings are booked for every weekday during the next sixty days."⁶⁷ Burgoo king Gus Jaubert claimed that he had "made more Democratic votes in the South than any other living man" with his burgoo.⁶⁸ The Missouri version of burgoo was believed to have similar powers. It was said that "no one ever heard of Missouri going Republican in a year when burgoo was on tap."⁶⁹

The Origin of Burgoo

Whatever the origin of the word *burgoo*, the details of the stew's origins are less murky. Kentuckians have been eating burgoo for a very long time. As one put it, burgoo goes back to the times "way before Henry Clay wore knee breeches."⁷⁰ According to at least one thankful burgoo enthusiast, whoever first cooked burgoo is greater than the person who invented the printing press.⁷¹

Some credit nineteenth-century burgoo king Gus Jaubert for inventing the stew in 1863.⁷² However, Jaubert denied such claims in spite of any temptation he may have had to claim greater glory than that given to Johannes Gutenberg.⁷³ In 1921, some theorized that French sailors introduced burgoo in the South before Kentuckians turned it into the Kentucky version of the stew.⁷⁴ It seems that the similarity of the word *burgoo* to the French word *ragoût* that refers to a strongly seasoned stew inclined some to believe that the French had something to do with originating the stew. The fact that Gus Jaubert was of French ancestry probably added credibility to the French origin theory.⁷⁵

Another old stew story holds that burgoo was an Indian stew recipe given to settlers by Native Americans. This theory is supported by the story that burgoo originally came from a recipe given to Daniel Boone by a man of French and Native American ancestry.⁷⁶ Similarly, others have claimed that burgoo is "a perpetual reminder of the aborigines (Native Americans) who handed it over to our pioneering forefathers when they began coming across the mountains from Virginia."⁷⁷

Sam Severance, a "burgoo master" who gained fame in 1940s Louisville, Kentucky, claimed that burgoo goes back to biblical times. According to him,

A Virginia Tradition

With tin cup in hand, everyone patiently waited to partake of the delicious burgoo simmering in large iron kettles at the Golden Jubilee held in Lexington, Kentucky, in 1916 to celebrate the fiftieth anniversary of the University of Kentucky. *Courtesy University of Kentucky.*

Esau traded his birthright for burgoo.[78] Brunswick stew masters have made similar claims. Perhaps this, too, is a holdover from Virginia soup feasts.

Some have tried to tie the origin of burgoo back to the Civil War. They argue that Gus Jaubert first cooked burgoo made with blackbirds for General John Hunt Morgan's cavalry.[79] Another claim is made that burgoo was first cooked in Kentucky around the year 1810 by a "Confederate cavalryman."[80] However, there were no Confederate cavalrymen in 1810. The date may be a typographical error and the cavalryman may be a reference to Gus Jaubert.

From Soup to Stew

The most plausible account of burgoo's origin holds that settlers from Virginia brought burgoo with them as they moved west into Kentucky County, Virginia, years before Kentucky became an independent state in 1792.[81] Some, including Gus Jaubert, claimed that the Virginians who brought burgoo to Kentucky were of Welsh descent. In 1899, an author for *The Epicure* wrote, "It seems that the idea of making burgoo came originally from Wales, but the Welsh product was rather a watery affair for the popular American taste, and it was only in Kentucky that burgoo arrived at its present rich consistency and delicious flavour by the added variety and quantity of its ingredients."[82]

In keeping with the descriptions of antebellum burgoo as being thin and soupy, a description of burgoo from 1859 describes it as "a kind of camp soup made of fish and turnips" seasoned with red pepper.[83] As eyewitnesses affirm, from colonial times to the start of the Civil War (the mid-1700s to mid-1800s), burgoo was not the rich, thick stew that we know today. In a description of burgoo from that era, the author explained, "The bergu [*sic*] was another great feast and consisted of five hundred squirrels properly cleaned and boiled to the consistency of soup in a twenty-gallon iron cauldron."[84] This account of the earliest burgoo recipe is amazingly similar to descriptions of Virginia's squirrel soup.[85] In an account of an antebellum burgoo that took place in Woodford, Illinois, we find a similar description of burgoo as a thin squirrel soup and not a stew as it is today:

> *In Walnut Grove there used to be immense numbers of squirrels, and in the early summer the people, for miles around would collect at the old meetinghouse spring on an appointed day, and enjoy what was called a "burgout." A burgout (pronounced burgoo) was a feast, the chief feature of which was squirrel soup. Early on the appointed day, the young men would be abroad with rifles, in search of young squirrels. By eight or nine o'clock these would begin to come in from all directions with their game. By this time, the old people and children had gathered together and the work of preparation was begun. Large kettles were suspended over the fire, and in these the dressed squirrels were deliciously souped. By the common consent, the direction of affairs was surrendered to Uncle "Lijah" Dickinson, who knew exactly how to make the best soup. The young man who brought in the greatest number of squirrels was the hero of the day, and divided the honor, if not the authority with Uncle Lijah. The soup was supplemented by the good things prepared at home, and the feast was always one of bounty and hospitality.*[86]

It is clear that burgoo and Brunswick stew traditions are rooted in the festive squirrel soup that resulted from farmers' efforts to protect their crops. In 1897, a writer discussed the history of burgoo and pointed out that it, like Brunswick stew, developed from squirrel soup cooked by hunters who lived in sparsely populated areas.[87] In 1871, people in Illinois used to hold burgoos that were essentially squirrel soup parties. Using the word *burgoo* as a verb, a newspaper reported, "When you 'burgoo,' you go into the woods somewhere with a big crowd of tip-top fellows, and have fun with the old boys. You commence with squirrel soup; then squirrels follow; then there is more soup; after which you take squirrels, and fall back on soup, and so keep things up."[88] Although tongue-in-cheek, this report supports the notion that just as Virginians improved squirrel soup to give us Brunswick stew, so Kentuckians improved squirrel soup to give us burgoo.

Burgoo Beyond Kentucky

Burgoo is a delicious dish with a long history, and its popularity has reached beyond Kentucky.[89] In 1903, hosts of a political barbecue in Columbus, Ohio, served what the newspaper called "Virginia burgoo."[90] One wonders if that dish was really burgoo or a misnamed Brunswick stew. In the 1950s, Mrs. Jouette Shouse regularly cooked five hundred gallons of burgoo for as many as two thousand guests at her estate (Wolf Trap Farm) in Fairfax, Virginia. Her burgoo recipe, described as a "squirrel dish," included squirrel meat, chicken and beef that was slowly simmered for at least eleven hours.[91]

By the end of the 1880s, it appeared that a strong Missouri (or "Mizzourah," as old newspapers spelled it) burgoo tradition was well on its way to being established.[92] In 1890, Senator Vest commented, "A native Missourian who doesn't know what burgoo is deserves to be transported to Kansas or Iowa." The people of Springfield, Illinois, liked burgoo so much that they chartered a burgoo club in 1877. The club lasted until sometime around the turn of the twentieth century.[93]

In 1885, Missouri politician Colonel John T. Crisp clipped a burgoo recipe from a newspaper and prepared what he called the first kettle of burgoo cooked in Jackson County, Missouri. Newspapers advertised the event as "A Burgout Feast" and described it as a "quaint festival held by old Kentuckians."[94]

Crisp's version of burgoo consisted of beef bones (for the marrow), twenty-five chickens, seventy-five squirrels, fifty squabs, twenty-five pounds of pork, twelve pounds of butter, fifteen pounds of ham, potatoes, onions, carrots, corn, macaroni, three hundred cayenne pepper pods and a large turtle. After hours of cooking, the burgoo was a rich burgundy color, and its aroma wafted for acres, drawing people "like flies around a honey jar." Each guest received a gallon "cup" three-fourths filled with burgoo topped off with croutons. Legend has it that long after eating Crisp's burgoo, people would "thereafter look upon other foods with contempt as only being capable of sustaining life."[95]

Newspaper reports claim that Crisp's "delectable and mysterious compound" required only a sip to "enslave a gourmet for life." Simmered for hours as Colonel Crisp supervised by sampling the burgoo as it cooked, the sublime stew would transform as the meat and vegetables "cooked to pieces" and blended into a "half solid, half liquid" culinary triumph that was "the final essence of all palatable nourishment." Now that's some high praise. There is no doubt that it fueled Crisp's boast that his Missouri burgoo surpassed any Kentucky version. Kentuckians took that statement as fighting words. Crisp's challenge was accepted by some fine Kentucky burgoo cooks, and the first burgoo cooking competition in history was set to take place about two miles outside Independence, Missouri, at Benton Park on September 4, 1885.[96] When Colonel Crisp died in 1903, the Missouri burgoo tradition almost died, too. A writer for the *Kansas City Star* asked in 1906, "Why no more burgoo?" and people there could only smack their lips over memories of "Mizzourah burgoo."[97]

Cities and towns all over Illinois have old burgoo traditions, too. This account of an Illinois burgoo reflects the influences of the old Virginia squirrel soup custom that still existed in the events as late as 1897:

> *The kettle is hung on a pole resting on 2 forks driven in the ground. The squirrels having been dressed and cleaned, are cut up and slated. They are then boiled and the scum taken off until the broth becomes clear. Then rice, sweet corn, tomatoes and other things used in soup, are added. The boiling is continued until the flesh leaves the bones, and all the ingredients are thoroughly cooked. The burgoo is then seasoned. Crackers and pickles are eaten with the soup, and ice cream, cake and lemonade finish the meal.*[98]

Arenzville, Illinois, claims to be the "home of the world's best burgoo."[99] In Scott County, Illinois, churches preserved a burgoo tradition until 1946, when the American Foreign Legion took it over. The Legion sponsored the annual burgoos from that time up until 1996, when it had to end the tradition due to lack of resources. Before it had to stop holding the burgoos, people called Winchester, Illinois, a "soup-crazy town."[100] The town of Winchester is again "soup-crazy"—in a good way, of course—after reviving its burgoo tradition in 2015.[101]

The Burgoo Kings

Kentuckians call most good burgoo cooks "burgoo masters." They reserve the most respected title "burgoo king" for only the greatest burgoo cooks.

Gustave Jaubert

Gustave (Gus) Jaubert (1838–1920) is Kentucky's most renowned burgoo king.[102] Born in New York in 1838, he moved with his French-born parents to Kentucky in 1842 when he was a young boy. He seemed to regret that he wasn't born in Kentucky. He often lamented, "If they'd [his parents] only started a little earlier I might have been a native-born Kentuckian."[103]

We have Gus Jaubert, the greatest Kentucky "burgoo man" in history, to thank for transforming burgoo from a thin squirrel soup into a rich stew. Similar to how James Matthews and Ned Stith turned squirrel soup into what we know today as Brunswick stew, after the end of the Civil War Gus Jaubert turned the soupy antebellum burgoo into a rich stew. He first cooked burgoo when he was a boy but was never happy with the result. In those days, according to Jaubert, burgoo recipes called for beef shank, chicken, corn, tomatoes, onions and some bacon. Immediately "after the [Civil] War," according to Jaubert, burgoo was still as "thin as dishwater."[104] He went on to say that "some of those early restaurant fellows would take a rooster that had reached the old-age limit and boil him in burgoo, spurs and all!"[105]

In 1852, caterers hired Jaubert to be head pit master at a barbecue held in Hopkinsville, Kentucky. That set him on his barbecue-cooking career. He interrupted his career as a "barbecuist" to serve as a soldier for four years during the Civil War. Initially, he served with the First Kentucky Infantry. Later, he joined John Morgan and participated in his famous raid throughout Ohio and Indiana.[106] Two of Jaubert's brothers also rode with Morgan but didn't survive the war.[107] Union soldiers eventually captured Jaubert in Ohio, and he spent the duration of the war incarcerated at Camp Douglas in Illinois.[108]

After the Civil War ended, Jaubert worked for two famous Kentucky barbecue cooks (Captain Beard and Jake Holstetter). After their deaths, he took over for them.[109] Jaubert used to feed tens of thousands of people in a single day with burgoo and barbecued pork, beef and mutton that he prepared with the help of his cooks.[110] He and his assistants cooked burgoo

> KENTUCKY'S CENTENNIAL CELEBRATION BILL OF FARE,
> PREPARED BY GUS JAUBERT, 1892
>
> | | | |
> |---|---|---|
> | 300 sheep | 100 hams | 100 shoats |
> | 6 bullocks | 15,000 loaves of bread | 30,000 gallons of burgoo |
> | 10 barrels of pickles | 50 dozen fat hens | 30 cases of tomatoes |
> | 20 cases of corn | 50 bushels of potatoes | 8 barrels of onions |
> | 10,000 tin cups | 10,000 spoons | salt & pepper |
> | 40 cords of wood | 20,000 feet of tables | 40 cooks |
>
> *Frankford Roundabout*, "Centennial Barbecue," May 28, 1892

for hours in immense iron kettles of three hundred to seven hundred gallons each. When done, cooks transferred the stew to clean tubs, and guests, armed with tin cups, would help themselves to the stew, taking as much as they desired.[111]

Jaubert believed that southern cooking was "too greasy" and always endeavored to improve it.[112] Before Jaubert's innovations, burgoo recipes called for middling or bacon, which reflects its roots in Virginia's squirrel soup.[113] Through experimentation, he made changes to the soupy version of burgoo, first by taking out the bacon and middling and increasing the amount of beef and chicken in addition to using potatoes as a thickener just as Virginians started using them to thicken Brunswick stew in the 1830s. He also highly seasoned his burgoo, which is testified to by the prominent number of "pods of red pepper" used in his recipe.[114] By 1866, he was serving his improved burgoo recipe at public gatherings, and people soon began calling it "Jaubert's Best."[115] It didn't take long for Jaubert to develop a national reputation for his barbecue and burgoo-cooking prowess. Besides Kentucky, he cooked all over the country, including in Ohio, Tennessee, Nebraska, Mississippi, Indiana, Wisconsin and Michigan.[116]

Jaubert never really shared his burgoo recipe. However, he, like James Tandy Ellis, opened up and admitted what wasn't in it. "Nobody but a crazy man ever puts whiskey in burgoo," Jaubert exclaimed before sharing the following recipe for making burgoo at home:

> *The kind of burgoo I make—the kind that has been drunk all over Kentucky, Indiana, and Ohio, is made of vegetables and meat alone. If you want to make, say a gallon of burgoo, take a gallon of water and put in a*

whole chicken and a beef shank cut up into small pieces. Keep this cooking until the meat is well done. Then put in four ears of corn, cut off the cob; half a dozen tomatoes, a dozen potatoes, three onions, all cut up very fine. This mixture must be stirred continuously to prevent scorching, and water must be added from time to time, as is necessary. It takes from two to three hours to cook burgoo properly, and when you take it off the stove it should be light brown in color and very thick.[117]

When Jaubert cooked for large events, the recipe was different than the one he shared for making burgoo at home. At one burgoo, he cooked four hundred pounds of beef, six dozen chickens, four dozen rabbits, thirty cans of tomatoes, twenty dozen cans of corn, fifteen bushels of potatoes and five bushels of onions all in a single iron kettle for twelve hours.

Well before daybreak, Jaubert and his assistants would fill his huge iron kettles about one-third full of water.[118] Then they added the beef and the chickens to the pots and boiled them until daybreak. At that point, they skimmed off the froth that formed on the surface of the liquid before removing all of the bones. The cooks would then add vegetables and seasonings, including plenty of red pepper, to the pot and simmer it for hours, after which the burgoo was ready to eat.[119] At the biggest events, Jaubert cooked several batches of burgoo. As servers emptied kettles in the morning, cooks filled the empty kettles again to make more burgoo for guests in the evening.[120]

The greatest barbecue and burgoo Jaubert ever cooked was held in Louisville, Kentucky, in September 1895. The occasion was an encampment of the Grand Army of the Republic, a national veterans association, where Jaubert cooked barbecue and burgoo for 200,000 people.[121] He cooked thirty thousand gallons of burgoo in fifteen kettles and barbecued 13 beeves (steers), 265 sheep and 240 shoats.[122] Jaubert had about 500 people working for him to assist with the work, 40 of whom carved the barbecued meat that was served on large, elliptical thirty- by twenty-inch platters.[123]

Sugar maple was Jaubert's wood of choice for cooking barbecue because he preferred the flavor it imparts. His cooks mopped the meat as it barbecued with melted suet that was kept simmering in a pot near the pits. Jaubert later recounted the biggest change at barbecues over his career, which was the fact that squirrels, rabbits and pigeons were often barbecued "in the old days" but those meats became too scarce to be cooked at big barbecues starting in the latter part of the nineteenth century. Jaubert preferred to cook whole animal carcasses because he believed it was easier to barbecue them

Burgoo King Gus Jaubert and his burgoo cooks in Lexington, Kentucky, in 1913. From *American Magazine*, December 1914. *Courtesy University of Michigan Library.*

that way. However, he preferred to quarter beef carcasses before barbecuing them.[124] As the meat barbecued, he kept "firemen" busy carrying buckets of water running along the barbecue pits putting out any flame-ups that might have started due to fat from the meat dripping in the coals.[125]

Jaubert had a huge seven-hundred-gallon iron pot in which he cooked burgoo for the largest events. Such kettles were so heavy they often required trains with derricks to transport and set them into place.[126] Foundry workers in Pittsburg cast Jaubert's massive seven-hundred-gallon kettle in 1805 for Neil McCoy's gunpowder mill. McCoy used it to make much of the gunpowder used by the early settlers in Kentucky and the gunpowder used by General Andrew Jackson at the Battle of New Orleans. Jaubert acquired it from McCoy's grandson Judge James H. Mulligan.[127]

Besides cooking at burgoos and barbecues, Jaubert also owned several businesses in his lifetime in addition to cooking for restaurants he didn't own. In the 1870 federal census, he listed his occupation as "saloon keeper."[128] The 1867 city directory for Lexington, Kentucky, lists Jaubert's "Magnolia Saloon, where everything suitable for the palate can be supplied," located at Short and Mulberry. Jaubert was also the proprietor of a saloon on Mill Street in Lexington, Kentucky, for thirty-seven years before he sold it in 1906 in favor of devoting more time to catering barbecues and burgoos.[129] An 1898 advertisement in a Lexington, Kentucky newspaper reads, "Burgoo at Gus Jaubert's from 10 to 12 a.m. today."[130] In 1903, another advertisement in the same newspaper read, "Burgoo every day this week at the Normandy. Made by Gus Jaubert."[131] He also sold "drink" at horse races.[132]

Jaubert married Emma Richards in 1868. They had seven children and remained happily married for fifty-two years until his death.[133] According to a warmhearted tribute printed in a Lexington newspaper after Jaubert's death in 1920, he was a very generous person. The tribute goes on to tell us that "he was honest as the day is long" and was "wont to send buckets of soup to the needy and suffering and how the poor newsboys came to your place and none left hungry…no one knows how many poor stranded souls lived on your bounty: for you never let your left hand know what the right one did."[134] One such event when Jaubert provided "buckets of soup to the needy" occurred in January 1893 during a particularly harsh winter. Jaubert cooked two hundred gallons of burgoo that he served free of charge to needy people in Lexington, Kentucky, made with beef, rice and turnips among the ingredients.[135]

Before Jaubert's last big barbecue and burgoo, catered in 1913 at Spring Hill farm near Versailles, Kentucky, for Senator Johnson N. Camden, he had conducted fifteen to twenty barbecues a year for almost fifty years.[136] In 1914, a Jaubert biographer estimated that if you took all of the burgoo cooked by Jaubert in his lifetime, it would make a burgoo lake sixty feet long, two hundred feet wide and six feet deep.[137] J.M. Benton of Winchester, Kentucky, lamented in 1929, nine years after Jaubert's death, "Unless Gus Jaubert's recipe can be resurrected I fear that the making of real burgoo is a lost art."[138]

Watson Green and Aaron Riggs: Jaubert's Assistant Cooks

The scale and scope of many of the barbecue and burgoo events catered by Jaubert make it clear that he wasn't personally cooking the food served to the guests. At those large events, Jaubert was supervisor more than cook. Many unnamed African Americans working behind the scenes contributed greatly to Jaubert's success. Two of those talented cooks were Watson Green and Aaron Riggs.

Watson Green (1827–1918?) was a "lard-sided, round-cheeked old King Cole of a cook" who was well known in and around Louisville after the close of the Civil War. He was born in Kentucky to Virginian parents. Green could cook "anything from old plantation dishes to French pâté." In 1876, Jaubert was the caterer for a barbecue and burgoo event in Louisville, Kentucky. Watson Green, along with his wife, Susan, and daughter, Ella, assisted Jaubert with the cooking.[139] After sampling a barbecued lamb cooked by Green for that event, an author wrote:

> *It was not meat; it was genuine, veritable double-distilled ambrosia.... The luscious brown flake, as it melted in my mouth, seemed to be the concentrated essence of all palatable juices.....Never did such a taste tickle my palate before; it was not a taste, it was a delicate aromatic aroma; a kind of freshly amen, which faded away on the palate so sweetly that you could hardly discern when it had ceased to be a flavor and become a remembrance.*[140]

Another cook employed by Jaubert was Aaron Riggs (1860?–1914). There is little doubt that Riggs's contributions to Jaubert's success were significant. Because he worked with Jaubert for several decades, Riggs was certainly a trusted employee and was integral in managing barbecues and burgoos catered by Jaubert until he died in 1914.[141] Because the end of Jaubert's career coincided with the decline of Riggs's health and his subsequent death, one must wonder if the loss of Riggs's assistance played a role in Jaubert's decision to retire.

Although they rarely received the credit they deserved, the African American cooks who assisted Jaubert were vital to his success. The lofty praises showered on Jaubert for his burgoo and barbecue testify to that fact.[142]

A Virginia Tradition

Nelson Dudley Lawrence

After Jaubert's retirement in 1913, Nelson Dudley Lawrence (1861–1931)—or "Dud," as friends affectionately called him—became "Lexington's premier burgoo maker."[143] Crowned "prince of burgoo makers" in 1909, he was at that time second only to the reigning king of burgoo cooks, Gus Jaubert. Lawrence would have to wait until Jaubert's retirement in 1914 to be Kentucky's burgoo king. In 1916, he was crowned Kentucky's new "king of barbecuists."[144]

Lawrence assisted Jaubert when he presided over his last big burgoo and barbecue event, hosted by Senator Johnson N. Camden at Spring Hill farm near Versailles, Kentucky, in 1913. Jaubert cooked the burgoo. Dud Lawrence served it with the help of sixty men, among whom were fifteen "well-trained" college students.[145]

Beginning in 1914, Lawrence replaced Jaubert as the chief burgoo and barbecue cook at Senator Camden's barbecues.[146] Cooking for political, private and charity events, Lawrence, like Jaubert, became famous for his burgoo outside of Kentucky.[147] In 1920, Lawrence cooked burgoo for forty thousand people in Jackson, Ohio. The burgoo included one thousand pounds of chicken, twenty-five bushels of cabbage, fifteen bushels of onions, seventy-five bushels of potatoes and one hundred bushels of tomatoes.[148]

"King of Barbecuists" Nelson Dudley Lawrence's burgoo crew at the Democratic Barbecue at Winchester, Kentucky, held in 1916. *Courtesy University of Kentucky Special Collections Research Center, Postcard Collection.*

James T. Looney

After Jaubert and Lawrence, the burgoo king mantle passed to James T. Looney (1869–1954), also known as Colonel Jim, of Lexington, Kentucky.[149] Looney learned to cook burgoo at around the turn of the twentieth century, first serving it at horse races.[150] He continued to cater burgoo events until about six months before he died at the age of eighty-four. Looney claimed that Gus Jaubert taught him to make burgoo.[151] If true, he may have received some burgoo lessons while at the racetrack. Jaubert was sometimes a bartender at horse races, making it possible that he and Looney collaborated in some way at those venues.

In 1932, Looney traveled to Atlanta in order to "prove that Brunswick stew doesn't compare with burgoo." There, he cooked enough burgoo for five hundred guests who attended the annual Atlanta Police Department's barbecue.[152] Although the burgoo was delicious, there is no evidence that Georgians traded their Brunswick stew for burgoo.

In the 1930s, people considered Looney to be an artist who used a ladle for a brush and a pot for a palette.[153] In those days, he used to cook burgoo at the Kentucky Derby. His secret recipe caused some to conjecture that he put everything into his burgoo but the horse.[154] However, a newspaper published his recipe for burgoo in 1948.[155] Instead of horsemeat, Looney made his version of burgoo with mutton. Looney declared, "You find no strings in my stew," which was another Looney innovation. Rather than just pulling the meat, letting it cook down into long strings, Looney removed the meat from the pot after it was tender, chopped it and returned it to the pot.[156]

In 1930, Colonel E.R. Bradley hosted a horse race for charity in Lexington, Kentucky. He hired Looney to cook his famous burgoo. Colonel Bradley was so impressed with Looney's stew he declared, "I wish especially the thank James T. Looney, the burgoo king, for the excellence of the food and the masterly manner in which he conducted the feeding arrangements today. In complement to him and to perpetuate his title, I am going to name a good two-year-old *Burgoo King*."[157]

Burgoo King won the Kentucky Derby in 1932.[158] He may be the most famous horse called by that name, but he wasn't the only one. A Kentucky racehorse named Burgout shows up in newspapers in 1839.[159] Newspapers in 1875 and 1876 also mention a racehorse named Burgoo.[160]

A Virginia Tradition

Daniel Carter Beard

Daniel Carter Beard (1850–1941) was born in Cincinnati, Ohio. He became a famous youth leader and author and was the national commissioner of the Boy Scouts of America. At around the turn of the twentieth century, Beard popularized his version of burgoo made by adding the liquid from canned olives just before serving it to guests. "If the Burgoo Master has attended strictly to his work," Beard explained, "the picnickers will find it one of the most delicious soups which they have ever tasted."

Declaring that "no two burgoos are alike," Beard's recipe required turtle meat, mutton and wild game, as well as tomatoes and myriad vegetables, although he specifically stated that beets and sweet potatoes are not allowed. He also decreed that ingredients purchased from the local butcher shop can make a tasty soup but "the 'goo isn't there. Consequently, you cannot call it a burgoo." He extolled the virtues of his burgoo served with an olive and a slice of lemon in the tin cup as "too good for any old King that ever lived."[161]

Daniel Carter Beard. Photo by George Grantham Bain. *Courtesy Library of Congress [LC-B2-1270-7].*

Elza Perry

For more than fifty years, the burgoo king Elza Perry (1877–1979) of Meredosia, Illinois, prepared burgoo for the people who lived in and around the Arenzville, Illinois area at their annual Homecoming festival. Burgoo aficionados who sampled Perry's burgoo declared, "Nobody can touch Elza" which was their way of saying that his burgoo is the best.[162]

Perry's burgoo was so famous that President Franklin Delano Roosevelt requested and received the recipe. Reportedly, the stew didn't impress the president. Illinois congressman James Barnes diagnosed the problem to be the electric stove on which the White House cook prepared it. In 1953, Perry shared his recipe with the world…at least part of it. His recipe calls for beef, chicken, cabbage, corn, celery, potatoes, tomatoes and other good things. Perry stressed that a wood fire and impeccable cleanliness are the two most important secrets to a delicious burgoo.[163]

South Carolina–Style Barbecue Sauce

INGREDIENTS
2 cups yellow mustard
1 cup of sugar
½ cup white distilled vinegar
salt, pepper and ground cayenne to taste

PREPARATION
Thoroughly mix all of the sauce ingredients together except the seasonings. Add the salt, pepper and cayenne to suit your taste. Makes about 20 ounces.

South Carolina–Style Barbecue Hash

INGREDIENTS
3 pounds of cubed beef
2 pounds of cubed pork
water, as needed
4 pounds chopped onions
1 stick of butter
salt, black pepper, cayenne pepper to taste
8 hours of moonlight (optional)

PREPARATION (REQUIRES FREQUENT STIRRING)
Cut the meat into ½- to ¾-inch chunks and add them to an 8-quart pot with a heavy-duty bottom. Add just enough water to cover the meat and place over medium heat. As soon as the water begins to simmer, remove the meat from the pot and drain it. Repeat this process two times.

Return the meat to the pot along with the chopped onions and fill with just enough water to cover. Simmer until the meat and onions are very tender. Stir often and add water as needed. Remove meat and onion from the pot and let them cool enough to handle. Put the broth into a bowl or grease separator and let it cool. Reserve the broth and discard the fat.

Once the meat and onions have cooled, chop them using a cleaver or a good knife. Make sure that no onion pieces remain recognizable. The texture of the meat should not be too chunky. Put the cooled meat and onions back into the pot with the broth. If needed, add just enough water to cover. While the meat and broth are cool enough to touch, use a potato masher or an electric hand mixer (my preferred tool for the job) to soften the meat. The idea is to stir many times in a few minutes rather than over a period of several hours. This will puree the onions while separating the individual meat fibers, giving the meat the proper texture.

Return the pot to a simmer and let the liquid in the stew reduce to reach a thick consistency with only a very little broth remaining, stirring often. Remove it from the heat source, add the butter and stir until it melts into the stew. Season to taste with salt, pepper and cayenne.

Without the barbecue sauce, this is a South Carolina Upcountry-style barbecue hash. For a Lowcountry-style hash, before serving, add barbecue sauce to suit your taste. The hash can be eaten alone or served over rice, grits, biscuits or barbecue. Makes 10 to 12 servings.

Central Virginia Barbecue Sauce

*This barbecue sauce is inspired by the sauce
my father used to make when I was a youngster.*

INGREDIENTS
1 cup tomato puree
1 cup distilled white vinegar
½ cup white or brown sugar
2 teaspoons curry powder (adjust to taste)
1 ½ teaspoons granulated onion (adjust to taste)
1 ½ teaspoons salt
1 teaspoon yellow mustard
1 teaspoon fine ground black pepper
ground cayenne pepper or red pepper flakes to taste

PREPARATION
Thoroughly mix all ingredients and refrigerate for 1 hour. Put sauce in a saucepan and slowly bring to a simmer over medium heat, stirring as needed. Remove from heat, cool and serve. Makes about 20 ounces of sauce.

A Virginia Tradition

Virginia-Style Barbecued Pork

In times past, Virginians barbecued pork directly over coals. The process takes many hours and lots of hard work to complete. This recipe is for the home cook who doesn't want to dig a pit in their backyard or spend hours tending a barbecue pit. The results are still delicious.

INGREDIENTS
2 tablespoons kosher salt
2 tablespoons coarse ground black pepper
1 tablespoon mild paprika
1 teaspoon red pepper flakes
2 pats of unsalted butter
¼ cup apple cider vinegar
1 8-pound pork butt

PREPARATION
Make the barbecue rub by thoroughly mixing the salt, pepper, paprika and red pepper flakes in a bowl. Apply a light coat of unsalted butter along with a few sprinkles of vinegar to the entire meat side surface of the pork butt. Follow that with a medium coat of rub. Barbecue the pork uncovered in an enclosed barbecue smoker at 275 degrees Fahrenheit for 3 hours. Use three to four hickory chunks for smoke. After 3 hours, tightly wrap the pork butt in two layers of aluminum foil and return it to the smoker. When the pork is tender, after about 3 to 4 hours, remove it from the smoker and let it rest for 30 minutes. The internal temperature of the pork butt should be at least 200 degrees Fahrenheit. However, don't go by temperature alone; tenderness is the true guide. Use the barbecue to make sandwiches topped with coleslaw and a little Virginia-style barbecue sauce. It is also delicious served with Indian hoecake. Serves 12 to 15 people.

Virginia-Style Hashed Barbecue

My father's barbecue hash inspired this recipe. It contains ingredients typical of the Virginia-style barbecue that I remember eating as a youngster. This recipe calls for pork; however, my father made it with beef on some occasions. Pull-tender roast pork or roast beef works well, too. Another option is to cook 1½ pounds of pork or beef as described in the South Carolina–style barbecue hash recipe without the onions and butter before adding the Virginia-style barbecue sauce.

Brunswick Stew

Ingredients
1 pound Virginia-style barbecued pork, chopped
salt and pepper to taste
1 ½ cups central Virginia–style barbecue sauce

Preparation
Simmer one pound of leftover barbecued pork over medium heat in just enough water to cover it. Stir often until most fibers in the meat are separated. Let the meat continue to simmer until most of the excess liquid has boiled away. Season with salt and pepper to taste. Add 1 ½ cups of central Virginia–style barbecue sauce and continue to simmer for ten minutes. Serve the hash with Indian hoecake or on heated hamburger buns. Serves 4 people.

Virginia Hoecakes

My mother made two styles of hoecakes. One consisted of wheat flour and the other (called "Indian hoecake") a mixture of wheat flour and unsweetened white cornmeal.

Ingredients
1 ½ tablespoons shortening (or lard)
1 cup self-rising flour
¼ cup plus 1 tablespoon of milk

Preparation
Add the shortening to the flour in a large mixing bowl. Using your fingers, cut in the shortening until you have small pea-sized pieces of it coated with flour. Add the milk to make a thick, moderately wet dough similar to pizza dough. If it's too sticky to handle in your hands, add a little more flour. If it's too dry, add a little more milk. Pinch off a golf ball–size piece of dough. Using your hands, flatten it into a ⅛- to ¼-inch-thick round cake. You should be able to make at least four 5-inch round hoecakes. Cook on a lightly greased pan or griddle over medium heat, flipping once. The hoecakes should be golden brown on both sides and fluffy in the center. Serve hot. For Indian hoecake, replace the flour with a mixture of ⅓ cup white, unsweetened cornmeal and ⅔ cup self-rising flour. Makes 4 hoecakes.

A Virginia Tradition

Virginia-Style Brunswick Stew Recipes for Large Batches

Stew master Chiles Cridlin of the Proclamation Stew Crew shares the following recipes for large batches of Virginia-style Brunswick stew. The Proclamation Stew Crew cooks thousands of gallons of Brunswick stew every year all around the Old Dominion in support of worthy causes.

Virginia-Style Brunswick Stew Large Batch Recipes				
yield in gallons	25	55	65	95
Ingredients	Quantity			
boneless, skinless chicken thighs (pounds)	60	120	160	200
fat back, aka "white meat" (pounds)	4	9	11	15
potatoes (pounds)	50	100	125	150
potatoes if pre-chopped (pounds)	40	80	100	140
onions (pounds)	25	50	60	100
onions if pre-chopped (pounds)	20	40	40	60
crushed tomatoes (no. 10 cans)	4	8	11	15
butter beans (no. 10 cans)	6	12	15	21
white shoepeg corn (no. 10 cans)	4	8	11	15
margarine or butter (pounds)	3	6	7	9
sugar (pounds)	2	4	4.5	6
salt (ounces)	10	26	29.5	36
black pepper (ounces)	2	4.5	5	7
cayenne pepper (ounces)	2	4.5	5	7

Preparation

These large batch recipes require constant stirring from beginning to end. The stew must be constantly stirred while it simmers. Moreover, the cook must constantly tend the cooking fire. When using propane to fuel the fire, it is common to have to turn the heat up or down or off at certain times throughout the cook. Keep an eye on the amount of heat. You shouldn't rapidly boil the stew. A slow simmer is best.

Finely chop the white meat and add it to the pot with the chicken. Add just enough water to cover and bring to a simmer. Let the meats

Brunswick Stew

simmer until the chicken easily falls apart. Add the potatoes, onions and ¼ of the seasonings. Bring to a simmer and cook until the potatoes are very soft. Add the tomatoes and ¼ of the seasonings and bring back to a simmer for thirty more minutes. If the stew becomes too thick during the cook, add a little water. Add the drained butterbeans and ¼ of the seasonings. Bring back to a simmer and cook until the beans are soft. Add the drained corn, butter and remaining seasonings. Cook for about 15 minutes longer. The stew is ready when the stirring paddle can stand up on its own in the pot. Like a good stew master, above all, make sure that you and your stew crew observe all safety precautions at all times.

NOTES

Chapter 1

1. R.T.W. Duke Jr., *The "Recollections" of R.T.W. Duke, Jr.*, UVa Special Collections Library, Duke Collection, 1899–1926.
2. Edward B. Tylor, "Fire, Cooking, and Vessels," in *Researches into the Early History of Mankind and the Development of Civilization* (London: John Murray, 1865), 262–63.
3. Arthur Schwartz, "Forward—From Sop to Soup to Supper," in *Soup Suppers: More than 100 Main-Course Soups and 40 Accompaniments* (New York: Harper Collins, 1994), 12.
4. Janet Clarkson, "Prologue," in *Soup a Global History* (London: Reaktion, 2010), 11.
5. Anne E. Yentsch and Julie Hunter, "West African Women, Food, and Cultural Values," in *A Chesapeake Family and Their Slaves: A Study in Historical Archaeology* (Cambridge, UK: Cambridge University Press, 1994), 205.
6. Helen C. Rountree, "Subsistence," in *The Powhatan Indians of Virginia: Their Traditional Culture* (Norman: University of Oklahoma Press, 1989).
7. Ibid., 51–52; Joseph R. Haynes, *Virginia Barbecue: A History* (Charleston, SC: The History Press, 2016).
8. Bruce Kraig, "Succotash," in *The Oxford Encyclopedia of Food and Drink in America*, vol. 1, ed. Andrew F. Smith (Oxford, UK: Oxford University Press, 2004), 374.
9. Saddler Taylor, "Brunswick Stew," in *The New Encyclopedia of Southern Culture*, vol. 7, 1st ed., ed. John T. Edge (Chapel Hill: University of North Carolina Press, 2007), 131–32.

10. Bernard W. Sheehan, "Dependence," in *Savagism and Civility: Indians and Englishmen in Colonial Virginia* (Cambridge, UK: Cambridge University Press, 1980), 104; Bill Deyo, "Patawomeck Indians of Virginia," Virginia's First People, http://virginiaindians.pwnet.org/today/patawomeck.php.

11. Virtual Jamestown, "Jamestown Artifacts," http://www.virtualjamestown.org/images/artifacts/jamestown.html.

12. Sandra L. Oliver, *Food in Colonial and Federal America* (Westport, CT: Greenwood Press, 2005).

13. "Cajun and Creole Food," in *The Oxford Encyclopedia of Food and Drink in America*, ed. Andrew F. Smith (Oxford, UK: Oxford University Press, 2004), 242; Merril D. Smith, *History of American Cooking* (Santa Barbara, CA: ABC-CLIO, 2013).

14. Mary Wallace Kelsey, "Beans of the Southwestern United States," in *Oxford Symposium on Food & Cookery, 1989: Staplefoods: Proceedings*, ed. Harlan Walker (London: Prospect Books, 1990), 126. Succotash was prepared by Indian tribes all over the United States. A Pueblo Indian version of succotash included chili peppers.

15. Frederick Douglass Opie, "Adding to My Bread and Greens," in *Hog & Hominy Soul Food from Africa to America* (New York: Columbia University Press, 2008), 21.

16. Libby H. O'Connell, "WPA Soup," in *The American Palate* (Illinois: Sourcebooks, 2014), 210–13.

17. *Post Crescent*, "A Supper with History," February 22, 1976; *Post Crescent*, "Turtle 'Booyah,'" May 15, 1928; *Duluth News-Tribune*, "Bovey Hunter Gives the Town Moose Meat Feast," November 27, 1912.

18. *Milwaukee Journal Sentinel*, "Bountiful Harvest Means It's Kermiss Time," September 11, 1968.

19. Ashley Steinbrinck, "The Real Reason We Call It Chicken Booyah in Wisconsin," WhooNEW, October 17, 2013, http://whoonew.com/2013/10/the-real-reason-we-call-it-chicken-booyah-in-wisconsin.

20. Mary Ann Defnet, "UW—Green Bay—Wisconsin's French Connections Origin of Booyah," University of Wisconsin–Green Bay, October 22, 1997, http://www.uwgb.edu/wisfrench/kitchen/booyalet.htm.

21. *Charlotte Observer*, "Social and Personal," November 6, 1908.

22. Gay Weeks Neale, *The Lunenburg Legacy* (Lunenburg Courthouse, VA: Lunenburg County Historical Society, 2005).

23. James Beard Foundation, *James Beard's All-American Eats: Recipes and Stories from Our Best-Loved Local Restaurants*, ed. Anya Hoffman (New York: Rizzoli, 2016).

Chapter 2

1. Marshall Wingfield, *Franklin County Virginia: A History* (Baltimore, MD: Clearfield, 2003).
2. L. Daniel Mouer, "Chesapeake Creoles: The Creation of Folk Culture in Colonial Virginia," *The Archeology of 17th-Century Virginia*, eds. Theodore R. Reinhart and Dennis J. Pogue (Richmond: Archeological Society of Virginia, 1993), 105–66.
3. Haynes, *Virginia Barbecue*.
4. J. Hammond Trumbull, "Words Derived from Indian Languages of North America," in *Transactions of the American Philological Association* (Hartford, CT: published by the association, 1873).
5. James A.H. Murray, ed., *A New English Dictionary on Historical Principles: Founded Mainly on the Materials Collected by the Philological Society*, vol. 1, part 2 (Oxford, UK: Clarendon Press, 1887), 1,148.
6. *Daily Courier*, "Mastodon Barbecue Intrigues Some," April 21, 1996.
7. *San Francisco Call*, "Restoring El Rancho," August 8, 1909.
8. *El Paso Herald*, July 18, 1914; Kenneth Mason, *African Americans and Race Relations in San Antonio, Texas, 1867–1937* (New York: Garland Pub., 1998); United States of America, Bureau of the Census. Twelfth Census of the United States, 1900 (Washington, D.C.: National Archives and Records Administration, 1900), T623, 1854 rolls; Thirteenth Census of the United States, 1910 (Washington, D.C.: National Archives and Records Administration microfilm publication), T624, 1,178 rolls.
9. Laughton Osborn, *The Magnetiser: The Prodigal Comedies in Prose* (New York: J. Miller, 1869).
10. *Harper's New Monthly Magazine* (April 1885).
11. Duke, *"Recollections."*
12. Norris Thaddeus, "Virginia Barbecues," *Forest & Stream* 5, no. 9 (October 7, 1875).
13. Duke, *"Recollections."*
14. Harriet Cushman, "The Parlor Car; Or, Jaunts of the Knock-About Club," *Christian Union*, October 27, 1887.
15. Marion Cabell Tyree, *Housekeeping in Old Virginia* (Louisville, KY: John P. Morton and Company, 1879). There is a Virginia barbecue recipe in this book that calls for tomato ketchup.
16. Gibson Jefferson McConnaughey, *Two Centuries of Virginia Cooking: The Haw Branch Plantation Cookbook* (Amelia, VA: Mid-South Publishing, 1977).

17. William Bullock, *Virginia Impartially Examined* (London: John Hammond, 1649).
18. Robert Beverly, *The History and Present State of Virginia*, Documenting the American South (N.p.: William S. Hein & Company, 2011).
19. Wilbur Fisk and Emil Rosenblatt, *Hard Marching Every Day: The Civil War Letters of Private Wilbur Fisk, 1861–1865* (Lawrence: University Press of Kansas, 1992), 27; William C. Davis, *A Taste for War: The Culinary History of the Blue and the Gray* (Mechanicsburg, PA: Stackpole Books, 2003), 50.
20. Marshall Fishwick, "Southern Cooking," in *American Heritage Cookbook & Illustrated History of American Eating and Drinking* (New York: Simon and Schuster, 1964).
21. Andrew F. Smith, ed., *The Oxford Companion to American Food and Drink* (New York: Oxford University Press, 2009); *Daughters of the American Revolution Magazine*, vol. 113 (Washington, D.C.: National Society of the Daughters of the American Revolution, 1979), 538; *Richmond Recorder*, "Stalled Beeves," April 6, 1803. "15000 weight of choice bacon, the hams salt-petered with particular care"; Smith, *History of American Cooking.*
22. Bullock, *Virginia Impartially Examined.*
23. John Clayton, *A Letter from Mr. John Clayton Rector of Crofton at Wakefield in Yorkshire, to the Royal Society, May 12, 1688* (Washington, D.C., 1836).
24. Hugh Jones, *The Present State of Virginia* (New York: reprinted for J. Sabin, 1865).
25. *Sunbury American and Shamokin Journal*, "Preservation of Bacon," May 15, 1841.
26. *Daily Dispatch*, "Mr. Jefferson's Hospitality," August 26, 1858.
27. *Times Sun*, "How to Cure an Old Virginia Ham," February 9, 1879.
28. *Alexandria Gazette*, "A Fish Fry in the Old Dominion," December 1, 1851.
29. John Smith, *Travels and Works of Captain John Smith*, part 1, ed. Edward Arber (New York: Burt Franklin, 1910).
30. Philip Vickers Fithian, "Journal & Letters of Philip Vickers Fithian 1773–1774: A Plantation Tutor of the Old Dominion," Gutenberg.org. June 20, 2012.
31. Henry C. Knight, *Letters from the South and West* (Boston: Richardson and Lord, 1824), 66.
32. Ferdinand M. Bayard and Ben C. McCary, *Travels of a Frenchman in Maryland and Virginia, with a Description of Philadelphia and Baltimore, in 1791* (Ann Arbor, MI: [Edwards Brothers], 1950).
33. *American Turf Register and Sporting Magazine*, "A Virginia Fish Fry" (August 1833).

34. *Richmond Times-Dispatch*, "Dreamy and Hazy Indian Summer," October 1, 1905.
35. Franklin F. Webb and Ricky L. Cox, *The Water-Powered Mills of Floyd County, Virginia Illustrated Histories, 1770–2010* (Jefferson, NC: McFarland & Company, Publishers, 2012), 142.
36. *Alexandria Gazette*, "Fish Fry in the Old Dominion."
37. Emory Dean Keoke and Kay Marie Porterfield, *American Indian Contributions to the World: 15,000 Years of Inventions and Innovations* (New York: Checkmark Books, 2003), 130; John Clark Ridpath, "The Catholic Endeavor," in *The New Complete History of the United States of America*, vol. 3 (Cincinnati, OH: Jones Brothers Publishing, 1912), 1,071; *City Gazette*, "Buckwheat Cakes," December 25, 1830; Rod Cofield, *How the Hoe Cake (Most Likely) Got Its Name*, Historic London Town and Gardens, 2008, http://www.historiclondontown.com/files/hoe-cake-etymology-web.pdf.
38. Thomas Anburey, *Anburey's Travels through the Interior Parts of America*, vol. 2 (Carlisle, PA: Applewood Books, 1970), 194.
39. Elizabeth E. Lea, "A Virginia Hoe Cake," in *Domestic Cookery Useful Receipts, and Hints to Young Housekeepers*, 10th ed. (Baltimore, MD: Cushings and Bailey, 1859), 81.
40. Fithian, "Journal & Letters of Philip Vickers Fithian."
41. A. Edlin, "To Make Indian Hoe Cake," in *A Treatise on the Art of Bread-Making Wherein the Mealing Trade, Assize Laws, and Every Circumstance Connected with the Art Is Particularly Examined* (London: printed by J. Wright for Vernor and Hood, 1805), 114.
42. *Sterling Daily Gazette*, "Lore of the Kitchen," April 10, 1888.
43. *Herald and Tribune*, June 3, 1880.
44. *Record Union*, "Alabama's Africa," May 24, 1890.
45. *Atlanta Constitution*, "Literature," July 28, 1901.
46. *Daily Times News*, "Flower Show—Tea," December 9, 1953.
47. *Virginia Gazette*, "To Be Sold at John Greenhow's Store," December 12, 1771; Oliver, *Food in Colonial and Federal America*.
48. Martha McCulloch Williams, *Dishes & Beverages of the Old South* (New York: McBride, Nast & Company, 1913).
49. *Richmond Whig*, "Hustings Court," May 24, 1850.
50. John Jay Janney, *John Jay Janney's Virginia: An American Farm Lad's Life in the Early 19th Century*, ed. Asa Moore Janney (McLean, VA: EPM Publications, 1978).
51. Smith, *Oxford Encyclopedia of Food and Drink in America*, 389.
52. Jacques Cartier, *The Voyages of Jacques Cartier*, ed. Ramsay Cook (Toronto: University of Toronto Press, 1993), 61.

53. Edward Eggleston, "Wild Flowers of English Speech in America," *Century Magazine* (April 1894).
54. Amelia Simmons, *American Cookery* (Bedford, MA: Applewood Books, 1996), 41. A recipe in this book is titled "Johnny Cake, or Hoe Cake," indicating that the names for the bread cakes are interchangeable. *Johnny cake* could be derived from the English word for oat cakes, *jannock*; Cofield, *How the Hoe Cake (Most Likely) Got Its Name*; Keith W.F. Stavely and Kathleen Fitzgerald, "Johnny Cake: Where It Came From," in *America's Founding Food the Story of New England Cooking* (Chapel Hill: University of North Carolina Press, 2004). Some claim that calling the cakes *journey cakes* comes from the corn cakes Indians used to take with them on journeys; Lea, "Virginia Hoe Cake," 81. The recipe for "A Virginia Hoe Cake" is almost identical to Randolph's Johnny cake recipe even down to the board set aslant before the fire.
55. *New England Kitchen Magazine*, "Seasonable Recipes—Including Some for Camping and Picnicking" (August 1895).
56. Mary Randolph, "Rice Journey, or Johnny Cake," in *The Virginia Housewife: Or, Methodical Cook*, stereotype ed. (Baltimore, MD: Plaskitt, Fite & Company, 1838); Smith, *Oxford Encyclopedia of Food and Drink in America*, 389.
57. Harrell Site, "What the Artifacts Tell Us," August 8, 2002, http://www.texasbeyondhistory.net/harrell/artifacts.html.
58. John Russell Bartlett, *Dictionary of Americanism: A Glossary of Words and Phrases Usually Regarded as Peculiar to the United States* (New York: Bartlett and Welford, 1848).
59. J. Howard Gore, "Tuckahoe, or Indian Bread," in *Annual Report of the Board of Regents of the Smithsonian Institution for the Year 1881* (Washington, D.C.: Smithsonian Institution, 1881).
60. Ibid.
61. *Daily Dispatch*, September 12, 1880; *Richmond Dispatch*, "Queries & Answers," November 20, 1892; *Richmond Dispatch*, "What Is a Tuckoe?," October 15, 1901.
62. William Wood, *Wood's New England's Prospect* (Boston: John Wilson and Son, 1865); Roger Williams, *A Key into the Language of America* (London: printed by G. Dexter, 1643).
63. Cofield, *How the Hoe Cake (Most Likely) Got Its Name*.
64. Keith W.F. Stavely and Kathleen Fitzgerald, *America's Founding Food: The Story of New England Cooking* (Chapel Hill: University of North Carolina Press, 2004).

65. John Smith, *The Trve Travels, Adventvres and Observations of Captaine Iohn Smith, in Europe, Asia, Africke, and America: Beginning about the Yeere 1593, and Continued to This Present 1629*, vol. 1 (Richmond, VA: republished at the Franklin Press, 1819).
66. *Evening Star*, "A Card," April 25, 1856.
67. William Strachey, *The Historie of Travaile into Virginia Britannia*, ed. Richard Henry Major (London: Hakluyt Society, 1849).
68. William Dunlap, *Diary of William Dunlap (1766–1839)* (New York: New York Historical Society, 1930).
69. "Lady," *A Poetical Picture of America Being Observations Made, during a Residence of Several Years, at Alexandria, and Norfolk, in Virginia: Illustrative of the Manners and Customs of the Inhabitants: And Interspersed with Anecdotes, Arising from a General Intercourse with Society in That Country, from the Year 1799 to 1807* (London: printed for the author by W. Wilson, 1809).
70. John Egerton and Ann Bleidt Egerton, "Pass and Repast," in *Southern Food: At Home, on the Road, in History* (New York: Knopf, 1987).
71. Rountree, "Subsistence," 51.
72. Sophie D. Coe, *America's First Cuisines* (Austin: University of Texas Press, 1994), 14; Daniel H. Usner, *Indians, Settlers & Slaves in a Frontier Exchange Economy: The Lower Mississippi Valley before 1783* (Chapel Hill: University of North Carolina Press, 1992), 205.
73. Karen Ordahl Kupperman, *The Atlantic in World History* (New York: Oxford University Press, 2012), 80; *Journal of American History* 66, no. 1 "Apathy and Death in Early Jamestown" (1979): 24–40.
74. Roon Frost, "High on the Hog in Virginia," *Gourmet—The Magazine of Good Living* (April 1981).

Chapter 3

1. *Harper's New Monthly Magazine*, "The Cosmopolite Bill of Fare" (April 1859).
2. John L. Koprowski, *Mammalian Species*, no. 480, "*Sciurus carolinensis*," December 2, 1994; Paul D. Curtis and Kristi L. Sullivan, *Wildlife Damage Management Fact Sheet Series*, "Tree Squirrels," 2001, Cornell Cooperative Extension, Wildlife Damage Management System, Ithaca, New York.
3. Ernest Ingersoll, *Our Gray Squirrels: A Study* (New York: Harper, 1892).
4. *Richmond Dispatch*, "The Idle Reporter's Reflections on Farmers," September 29, 1901.

5. *Free Lance Star*, July 21, 1906.
6. *Monthly Bulletin* 7 (November–December 1918), California State Commission of Horticulture.
7. John D. Godman, *American Natural History*, vol. 2, part 1, *Mastology* (Philadelphia, PA: Key & Mielkie, 1831).
8. John Bradbury, *Travels in the Interior of America, in the Years 1809, 1810, and 1811* (London: Sherwood, Neely, and Jones, 1817).
9. *Alexandria Herald*, "Squirrels," November 11, 1822.
10. *Spooner's Vermont Journal*, "Grand Squirrel Hunt," October 14, 1822.
11. *Richmond Enquirer*, "Grand Squirrel Hunt," November 22, 1836.
12. *Virginia Argus*, "A Squirrel Hunt," October 15, 1803.
13. *Daily Advisor*, May 8, 1805.
14. Godman, *American Natural History*; John James Audubon and John Bachman, *The Viviparous Quadrupeds of North America*. London: Wiley and Putnam, 1847.
15. H.R. McIlwaine, *Journals of the House of Burgesses of Virginia, 1727–1734, 1736–1740* (Richmond, VA: Colonial Press, E. Waddey, 1910).
16. William Waller Hening, *The Statutes at Large; Being a Collection of All the Laws of Virginia, from the First Session of the Legislature, in the Year 1619*, vol. 13 (Richmond, VA: printed by and for Samuel Pleasants Jr., printer to the Commonwealth, 1809).
17. Thomas Forehand, *Robert E. Lee's Lighter Side: The Marble Man's Sense of Humor* (Gretna, LA: Pelican Pub. Company, 2006).
18. *Saturday Evening Post*, "Home Life of Garfield and Arthur," October 1, 1910.
19. *Tampa Tribune*, "Col. W.H. Crook, of White House, Dead," March 14, 1915; *Boston Herald*, "A Red Letter Day," September 3, 1881.
20. *Lexington Herald*, "Squirrelly Situation," July 8 1958.
21. *Lexington Herald*, "Blades of Blue Grass," May 9, 1937.
22. *Morning Advocate*, "Foodless 53-Days Ended as Faster Consumes Broth," May 2, 1937.
23. William Whitney, ed., *The Century Dictionary and Cyclopedia*, vol. 7 (New York: Century, 1897). One definition of the word *soup* in this dictionary is, "A kind of picnic in which a great pot of soup is the principal feature."
24. *Boston Cooking School Magazine*, "Home Ideas and Economies" (January 1, 1907): 97–99; Daniel Carter Beard, *The Jack of All Trades Fair Weather Ideas* (New York: C. Scribner's Sons, 1904), 107–10.
25. Otis K. Rice and Stephen Wayne Brown, *West Virginia a History*, 2nd ed. (Lexington: University Press of Kentucky, 1993).

26. *The Sun*, "Kissing Soup Parties in Virginia," August 10, 1899.
27. Lina Beard and Adelia B. Beard, *How to Amuse Yourself and Others: The American Girls Handy Book* (New York: Charles Scribner's Sons, 1893), 132–34.
28. *Richmond Times-Dispatch*, "Personal and General," June 18, 1907.
29. *Richmond Times-Dispatch*, "On-Looker in the Market," August 16, 1903.
30. *Alexandria Gazette*, "A Brunswick Stew," June 26, 1855.
31. *Indianapolis News*, "Virginia Ham and Virginia Cooking," October 6, 1905.
32. Mary Virginia Terhune, *Marion Harland's Complete Cook Book: A Practical and Exhaustive Manual of Cookery and Housekeeping, Containing Thousands of Carefully Proved Recipes*, 1831–1922, new ed., rev. and enl. (Indianapolis, IN: Bobbs-Merrill Company, 1906).
33. *American Law Review*, September–October 1903.
34. *Lexington Herald*, December 2, 1930.
35. Irvin Bacheller, *Everybody's Magazine*, "A Man for the Ages" (August 1919).
36. *Indiana Magazine of History* 2, no. 1, "Squirrel 'Burgoo'" (March 1906).

Chapter 4

1. Philip Alexander Bruce, *Economic History of Virginia in the Seventeenth Century: An Inquiry into the Material Condition of the People* (New York: Macmillan, 1896); Betty Wason, *The Language of Cookery: An Informal Dictionary* (Cleveland, OH: World Pub. Company, 1968); Alice Morse Earle, *Home Life in Colonial Days* (New York: Macmillan Company, 1898).
2. Susan Dosier, "Meats of North America," in *Colonial Cooking* (Mankato, MN: Blue Earth Books, 2000), 24.
3. *Augusta Chronicle*, "The Barbecue," July 2, 1840.
4. Duke, *"Recollections."*
5. *Macon Telegraph*, "Just 'Twixt Us," July 19, 1920.
6. Kathleen Purvis, *Rome News Tribune*, "On Family Tree of Barbecue, Hash Is a Strange Stump," July 14, 1999; *Augusta Chronicle*, "An Excursion to Augusta, Ga.," May 11, 1890.
7. *Catoctin Clarion*, "Home of the Barbecue," May 19, 1887; *Macon Telegraph*, "Just 'Twixt Us."
8. *Edgefield Advertiser*, "Some Modern Definitions," December 13, 1911.
9. Alexander Edwin Sweet and J. Armoy Knox, *On a Mexican Mustang, through Texas, from the Gulf to the Rio Grande* (Hartford, CT: S.S. Scranton & Company, 1883), 315.

10. William Kitchiner, *The Cook's Oracle: Containing Receipts for Plain Cookery on the Most Economical Plan for Private Families* (London: printed for Robert Cadell, Edinburgh, 1831).
11. *Good Housekeeping*, "Hash," January 23, 1886.
12. J. Rosalie Benton, *How to Cook Well* (Boston: D. Lothrop & Company, 1886), 31.
13. Esther Copley, "Hashes," in *The Housekeeper's Guide; Or, A Plain and Practical System of Domestic Cookery* (London: Jackson and Walford, 1838).
14. *Good Housekeeping*, "Hash," January 23, 1886.
15. Ibid.
16. *Dwight's American Magazine, and Family Newspaper*, "Hash," April 17, 1847.
17. *Macon Telegraph*, "Just 'Twixt Us."
18. John S. Farmer, *Slang and Its Analogues Past and Present* (N.p.: Harrison & Sons, 1893).
19. John M. Dagnall, *Our American Hash: A Satire in Prose and Verse* (New York: published by the author, 1880).
20. *Puck*, "Confessions of a Hash-Eater," March 10, 1886.
21. *New York Times*, "The Sunny South Invaded," May 13, 1890.
22. *Yorkville Enquirer*, "Letter from Chester," August 14, 1889.
23. *Catoctin Clarion*, "Home of the Barbecue," May 19, 1887; *Macon Telegraph*, "Just 'Twixt Us."
24. *Independent Press*, "Plantation Barbecues," July 27, 1860.
25. Joel Chandler Harris, *Mr. Rabbit at Home: A Sequel to "Little Mr. Thimblefinger and His Queer Country"…Illustrated by O. Herford* (London: Osgood, McIlvaine & Company, 1895), 86. Although this book is a work of fiction, it does describe real-world events. One event was a barbecue where barbecue hash was served made of lamb and hog "giblets"; John Egerton and Ann Bleidt Egerton, *Southern Food: At Home, on the Road, in History* (New York: Knopf, 1987).
26. Z.F. Smith, *The History of Kentucky from Its Earliest Discovery and Settlement, to the Present Date* (Louisville, KY: Prentice Press, 1895), 371.
27. James Mooney, *The Ghost-Dance Religion and the Sioux Outbreak of 1800* (Washington, D.C.: Government Printing Office, 1896), 1,067.
28. John Lawson, "A New Voyage to Carolina," Project Gutenberg, 1711.
29. E. Laveille and Marian Lindsay, *The Life of Father De Smet, S.J. (1801–1873)* (New York: P.J. Kenedy & Sons, 1915), 184.
30. *Danville Bee*, July 26, 1924; *Daily Dispatch*, "Local Matters," June 19, 1852—pigs' head hash was served at a Virginia barbecue in Richmond; *Fredericksburg Herald*, July 9, 1855—shoat hind hash was served at a barbecue in Fredericksburg.

31. *Woman's Auxiliary of Olivet Episcopal Church. Virginia Cookery, Past and Present: Including a Manuscript Cook Book of the Lee and Washington Families Published for the First Time* (Franconia, VA: Woman's Auxiliary of Olivet Episcopal Church, 1957).
32. *Daily Journal*, "Celery to Day," October 13, 1912; *Gastonia (NC) Gazette*, April 4, 1949; *Daily Phoenix (AZ)*, "Local Items," September 19, 1871; *El Paso Evening Post*, June 13, 1928. The El Paso Barbecue restaurant advertised "Barbecue Beef, Barbecue Hash" on the menu.
33. *Ashville Citizen-Times*, April 1, 2016.
34. *Washington Bee*, "Killed by Barbecue Hash," September 27, 1902.
35. Bradley Robert Rice and Harvey H. Jackson, "Castleberry's Food Company," in *Georgia: The Empire State of the South* (Brightwaters, NY: Windsor Publications, 1988). One of the first products canned by Castleberry's food company in 1926 was Georgia Barbecue Hash.
36. *Atlanta Constitution*, "Delighted with Dixie," July 15, 1884.
37. *Catoctin Clarion*, "Home of the Barbecue," May 19, 1887.
38. Cora Brown and Rose Brown, "Georgia Barbecue Hash," in *America Cooks: Practical Recipes from 48 States* (New York: W.W. Norton, 1940), 134.
39. Benton, *How to Cook Well*, 28.
40. McConnaughey, *Two Centuries of Virginia Cooking*, 106, 112.
41. Clarrissa Dillon, "A Hog Drest Whole: Early Barbecue References," *Food History News* (Fall 1995). Sandra L. Oliver has my gratitude for her assistance in helping me acquire a copy of this edition of this out-of-print periodical. The old Philadelphia barbecue recipe was found by Dr. Dillon in "The Receipt Book of Elizabeth Coates Paschall," unpublished manuscript, collection of the College of Physicians of Philadelphia, page 86.
42. *Kansas City Star*, October 1, 1940; *Trenton Evening Times*, "Barbecue Hash," April 1, 1948; *Bellingham Herald*, "Barbecue Hash and Rice New," July 6, 1950; *Greensboro Record*, "Carolina Cookery," October 15, 1953; *Boston Herald*, "Favorite Recipes," September 6, 1963; *Trenton Evening Times*, "Barbecue Hash," April 1, 1948.
43. *Recipes for Quantity Service*, no. 238 (1954), U.S. Department of Agriculture Extension Service, Program Aid.
44. *Abbeville Press and Banner*, October 15, 1884.
45. Purvis, "On Family Tree of Barbecue."
46. Lake E. High, "Time Out for Hash," in *A History of South Carolina Barbeque* (Charleston, SC: The History Press, 2013), 103.

47. Saddler Taylor and Stan Woodard, "South Carolina Hash," in *The New Encyclopedia of Southern Culture*, vol. 7, ed. John T. Edge (Chapel Hill: University of North Carolina Press, 2007), 179–81.
48. Saddler Taylor, "Hash," in *The South Carolina Encyclopedia*, ed. Walter B. Edgar (Columbia: University of South Carolina Press, 2006), 432–33.
49. *Index Journal*, August 22, 1919.
50. *Coffee and Tea Industries and the Flavor Field*, May 1920.
51. *Alexandria Gazette*, September 5, 1900; *Free Lance Star*, June 14, 1900.
52. *Philadelphia Inquirer*, "King Barbecuer Honors M'Kinley," September 5, 1900.

Chapter 5

1. Marion Harland, *Autobiography: The Story of a Long Life* (New York: Harper & Brothers, 1910).
2. *Daily Notes*, "Brunswick Stew," May 7, 1906.
3. *Indianapolis News*, "Virginia Ham and Virginia Cooking," October 6, 1905. This article was originally printed in the *Richmond Times-Dispatch*.
4. *Times Dispatch*, "Brunswick Stew," May 22, 1903.
5. *The Bee*, March 26, 1926.
6. *New York Herald*, "The Old Fashioned Barbecue in Virginia," April 29, 1858; *Richmond Times-Dispatch*, "Brunswick Stew Is a Famous One-Dish Meal," July 4, 1965.
7. *Richmond Whig*, "A Book on Fishing," April 20, 1869.
8. *Palm Beach Post*, October 28, 1982.
9. *Evening News*, "The Political Barbecue," September 11, 1905.
10. *Irish American Weekly*, "Florida 'Brunswick Stew,'" September 13, 1879; *Edwardsville Intelligencer*, "About that 'Kentucky Burgoo,'" October 14, 1969.
11. *Progress Index*, "Many Claim Invention of First Brunswick Stew," October 11, 1953.
12. *Saginaw News*, "Brunswick Stew," October 18, 1898.
13. *San Francisco Call*, "Brunswick Stew," January 7, 1912; Bruce Kraig, "Brunswick Stew," in *Oxford Encyclopedia of Food and Drink in America*, vol. 1, ed. Andrew F. Smith (Oxford, UK: Oxford University Press, 2004), 222.
14. *Brooklyn Daily Eagle*, "A Georgia Barbecue," October 27, 1898.
15. Mark F. Sohn, *Appalachian Home Cooking: History, Culture, and Recipes* (Lexington: University Press of Kentucky, 2005); Linda Garland Page,

The Foxfire Book of Appalachian Cookery (Chapel Hill, NC: University of North Carolina Press, 1992).
16. *Progress Index*, "Many Claim Invention of First Brunswick Stew"; *El Paso Herald*, "Pioneers' Day Is Proclaimed Holiday," November 13, 1914; *Paducah Evening Sun*, "The Local News," October 15, 1908.
17. Haynes, *Virginia Barbecue*.
18. *Harrisonburg Rockingham Register*, "East Rockingham Barbecue," August 22, 1873; *Times Dispatch*, "Brunswick Stew," May 22, 1903; *Boston Daily Advertiser*, August 31, 1891.
19. *Colorado Springs Gazette*, "A Brunswick Stew," July 8, 1907.
20. *Daily Notes*, "Brunswick Stew."
21. *Clarion*, June 9, 1886.
22. *Alexandria Gazette*, "An 'Old Virginia' Barbecue," September 14, 1849.
23. *Progress Index*, "The Brunswick Stew," September 15, 1957; *Daily Notes*, "A Gastronomic Triumph with a National Reputation," May 7, 1906; *Richmond Times-Dispatch*, "Plan Annual Picnic," June 26, 1927; Virginia Federation of Home Demonstration Clubs, *Recipes from Old Virginia* (Richmond, VA: Dietz Press, 1946).
24. *Richmond Times-Dispatch*, "Mixing Bowl," August 1, 1942.
25. Halstead Clotworthy Fowler, Dorothy Wagner and George Dewey Vanture, "Virginia Brunswick Stew," in *Recipes Out of Bilibid* (New York: G.W. Stewart, Publisher, 1946), 23.
26. Ginter Park Women's Club, *Famous Recipes from Old Virginia*, 2nd ed. (Richmond, VA: [C.W. Saunders], 1941), 80.
27. Christy Campbell, *Eat & Explore Virginia*, 1st ed. (N.p.: Great American Publishers, 2012), 45.
28. Cora Brown and Rose Brown, *America Cooks: Practical Recipes from 48 States* (New York: W.W. Norton &, 1940), 837.
29. *Richmond Times-Dispatch*, "Stew's Star of King and Queen Fair," October 7, 1982.
30. *Richmond Whig*, "A Virginia Stew," August 15, 1862; *Richmond Times-Dispatch*, "Brunswick Stew," April 4, 1906; League of Women Voters of Virginia, *Virginia Cookery Book: Traditional Recipes* (Richmond: Virginia League of Women Voters, 1921); *Daily Notes*, "Brunswick Stew."
31. *Times Dispatch*, "Brunswick Stew," May 22, 1903.
32. Mary Stuart Smith, comp., *Virginia Cookery-Book* (New York: Harper & Brothers, 1885), 108.
33. *Richmond Dispatch*, "Elks Have a Barbecue in Albemarle," August 16, 1902; Duke, *"Recollections"*; Women's Centennial Executive Committee,

"A Virginia Brunswick Stew," in *The National Cookery Book*, ed. Elizabeth Duane Gillespie (Bedford, MA: Applewood Books, 2005), 138. The 1876 recipe for Brunswick stew in this book includes okra.

34. *Richmond Times-Dispatch*, "The Brunswick Stew," January 19, 1908.
35. Ibid., "The Art of the Stew," December 15, 1946.
36. *Richmond Dispatch*, "Brunswick Stew," June 14, 1891.
37. Tyree, *Housekeeping in Old Virginia*.
38. Carrie Pickett Moore, *The Way to the Heart: Hints to the Inexperienced; a Collection of Tested Virginia Recipes* (Richmond, VA: Whittet & Shepperson, 1905), 11.
39. Ginter Park Women's Club, *Famous Recipes from Old Virginia*, 80.
40. *Jasper News*, "Virginia Brunswick Stew," February 19, 1920.
41. Jennifer V. Cole, "Who Makes the Best Brunswick Stew?," *Southern Living* (October 1, 2009).
42. *Richmond Dispatch*, "Brunswick Stew," June 14, 1891.
43. Charles H. Gibson, *Mrs. Charles H. Gibson's Maryland and Virginia Cook Book* (Baltimore, MD: J. Murphy & Company, 1894).
44. *Richmond Dispatch*, "Brunswick Stew," June 14, 1891.
45. *Janesville Daily Gazette*, "A Toothsome Oddity in Eating," January 21, 1887; *Washington Herald*, "Dishes with an Autumn Flavor," November 19, 1912; Jim Shahin, "Brunswick Stew, the Virginia Way," *Washington Post*, January 7, 2014, http://www.washingtonpost.com/lifestyle/food/brunswick-stew-the-virginia-way/2014/01/06/38e27446-6e4f-11e3-a523-fe73f0ff6b8d_story.html; Virginia Federation of Home Demonstration Clubs, *Recipes from Old Virginia*; Ginter Park Women's Club, *Famous Recipes from Old Virginia*, 63.
46. *Richmond Times-Dispatch*, "It Isn't Brunswick," January 16, 1947.
47. *El Paso Herald*, November 13, 1914.
48. *Fort Worth Morning Register*, "Hopkins County Stew," June 10, 1901. The recipe for Hopkins County stew in this article is identical to Virginia Brunswick stew recipes of the same era.
49. Robert E. Thomas, *The Thomas Family in 300 Years of American History* (Dallas, TX: Thomas, 1978), 164.
50. *Dallas Morning News*, "Hopkins County to Dish Stew for Home-Coming," June 27, 1954.
51. Jessie S. Grigg, "Knife and Fork," *State, Down Home in North Carolina* 39, no. 13 (December 1, 1971).
52. *Greensboro Daily News*, "Flowering of Brunswick Stew," November 11, 1954.

53. *Catoctin Clarion*, "Home of the Barbecue," May 19, 1887.
54. *Winchester News*, "Atlanta Ready to Greet Taft," January 15, 1909.
55. Rufas Jarman, "Dixie's Most Disputed Dish," *Saturday Evening Post*, July 3, 1954, 36–37, 89–91.
56. *Oregonian*, "The Epicure," November 16, 1947.
57. *Wichita Daily Eagle*, "An Old Time Southern Festivity that Is Passing Away," June 29, 1894.
58. *Richmond Times-Dispatch*, "The Art of the Stew," December 15, 1946.
59. *Brooklyn Daily Eagle*, "A Georgia Barbecue," October 27, 1898.
60. Lucy C. Andrews, "Southern Prize Recipes," *American Kitchen Magazine* (February 1, 1897).
61. *Macon Telegraph*, "Just 'Twixt Us."
62. John Farley, *The London Art of Cookery and Housekeeper's Complete Assistant. On a New Plan. Made Plain and Easy*, 9th ed. (London: printed by John Barker, for James Scatcherd, 1800), 74; Adolphe Gallier, "Chicken Hash with Cream," in *The Majestic Family Cook-Book: Containing 1300 Selected Recipes, Simplified for the Use of Housekeepers, Also a Few Choice Bills of Fare* (New York: G.P. Putnam's Sons, 1897), 247.
63. *Harper's Weekly*, "The Georgia Barbecue" (November 9, 1895).
64. *Piqua Daily Call*, "4th in Old Virginia," June 21, 1897; *Progress Index*, "Many Claim Invention of First Brunswick Stew."
65. *Richmond Times-Dispatch*, "The Brunswick Stew," January 19, 1908.
66. *Times Dispatch*, "Brunswick Stew," May 22, 1903.
67. *Atlanta Journal*, April 28, 1946.
68. *New York Times*, "Fare of the Country; Who Invented Brunswick Stew? Hush Up and Eat," October 24, 1993; Georgia's Golden Isles & Colonial Coast, "World Famous Brunswick Stew," http://www.officialguide.com/gistew.html.
69. *Brunswick Stew: Georgia Named Her; Georgia Claims Her*, Woodward Studio Ltd., 2005, DVD.
70. *Savannah Morning News*, "Brunswick Stews Battle Simmers Fight between Georgia," November 2, 2001, http://savannahnow.com/stories/110201/LOCstew.shtml.
71. Rufas Jarman, "Dixie's Most Disputed Dish," in *Cornbread Nation 2: The United States of Barbecue*, ed. Lolis Eric Elie (Chapel Hill: University of North Carolina Press, 2004), 41.
72. Ibid., "Dixie's Most Disputed Dish," *Saturday Evening Post*, 36–37, 89–91.
73. Harland, *Autobiography*; *Richmond Dispatch*, "Old Time Politics," August 10, 1892.

74. Women's Centennial Executive Committee, "A Virginia Brunswick Stew," 138.
75. *Macon Telegraph*, "Brunswick Stew," August 19, 1886.
76. *Janesville Daily Gazette*, "A Toothsome Oddity in Eating."
77. *Savannah Daily Advertiser*, "Lunch," July 1, 1871.
78. A.P. Hill and Damon Lee Fowler, "Camp Stew—Mr. B.'s Receipt," in *Mrs. Hill's Southern Practical Cookery and Receipt Book* (Columbia: University of South Carolina Press, 1995), 68.
79. Marjorie Kinnan Rawlings, "Game and Meats," in *Cross Creek Cookery* (New York: Charles Scribner's Sons, 1942).
80. *Southern Recorder*, "Virginia Stew," September 2, 1862; Andrew F. Smith, "Brunswick Stew," in *The Oxford Encyclopedia of Food and Drink in America* (Oxford, UK: Oxford University Press, 2013), 222; Rick McDaniel, *An Irresistible History of Southern Food: Four Centuries of Black-Eyed Peas, Collard Greens & Whole Hog Barbecue* (Charleston, SC: The History Press, 2011), 131.
81. J.L. Herring, *Saturday Night Sketches: Stories of Old Wiregrass Georgia* (Boston: Gorham Press, 1918), 229.
82. *Times Dispatch*, "Recollections of a Youthful Rebel," February 12, 1911.
83. *Adams Sentinel*, "What Soldiers' 'Snacks' Are Made Of," August 11, 1863.
84. David Hackett Fischer and James C. Kelly, *Bound Away: Virginia and the Westward Movement* (Charlottesville: University Press of Virginia, 2000).
85. Haynes, *Virginia Barbecue*.
86. John A. Burrison, "Brunswick Stew," New Georgia Encyclopedia, August 16, 2013, http://www.georgiaencyclopedia.org/articles/arts-culture/brunswick-stew.
87. *Richmond Times-Dispatch*, "The Home of Brunswick Stew," May 7, 1946; Gay Weeks Neale and Henry L. Mitchell, *Brunswick County, Virginia, 1720–1975* (Brunswick County, VA: Brunswick County Bicentennial Committee, 1975), 154–56.
88. *Savanah Morning News*, "Virginia's Brunswick Stew Trophy Turns Up in Georgia," October 14, 1999.
89. Taste of Brunswick Festival, "History," http://www.tasteofbrunswickfestival.com/history.html.
90. Printed in an article from an unidentified publication stored in the Isle of Wight County Museum's archives titled "Smithfield's People and Products."
91. *Richmond Times-Dispatch*, "Horace Hilliard Heartwell," March 24, 1916.
92. *Greensboro Daily News*, "Justices Entertain at Idlewood Home," July 19, 1927.

93. *Richmond Times-Dispatch*, July 4, 1965.
94. *The Times*, "How to Make Old Virginia Brunswick Stew," August 11, 1901; *Richmond Times-Dispatch*, May 7, 1946.
95. *Richmond Times-Dispatch*, "Officials Stew in Brunswick," November 17, 1978.
96. *Richmond Times-Dispatch*, "Another Look at a Stew Steeped in Controversy," December 11, 1978.
97. Taste of Brunswick Festival, "History."
98. *Daily Notes*, "Brunswick Stew."
99. *Macon Telegraph*, August 19, 1886.
100. *Times-Dispatch*, "The Stith Family of Virginia," April 17, 1904.
101. *Brunswick Times-Gazette*, "What Was Brunswick County Like Before Fort Christanna?," October 22, 2013.
102. R.A. Brock and Virgil Anson Lewis, *Virginia and Virginians: Eminent Virginians, Executives of the Colony of Virginia*, vol. 2 (Richmond, VA: H.H. Hardesty, 1888).
103. I.E. Spatig, "The Brunswick Stew," in *Brunswick County, Virginia* (Richmond, VA: Williams Printing Company, 1907).
104. *Richmond Times-Dispatch*, "The Taste Lingers On," December 20, 1946.
105. *Boston Daily Advertiser*, "The Breakfast Table," August 31, 1891.
106. *Palm Beach Post*, "Brunswick Stew the Choice for 1-Dish Meal for Crowd," October 28, 1982.
107. Louis A. Spievak, "Brunswick Stew," in *Barbecue Chef: Manual of Barbecue Parties, Recipes, Equipment* (Los Angeles, CA: L.A. Spievak Corporation, 1950), 54; Grigg, "Knife and Fork."
108. *Enquirer*, "Died," January 21, 1848.
109. *Richmond Enquirer*, "Huguenot Springs," June 5, 1846.
110. *Daily Dispatch*, "Barbecue," April 11, 1853; *Daily Dispatch*, October 29, 1853; *Daily Dispatch*, "Manchester and Vicinity," August 5, 1881.
111. *Enquirer*, "Rough Notes," September 14, 1849.
112. Spatig, "Brunswick Stew."
113. *Richmond Times Dispatch*, "The Mixing Bowl," September 1, 1938.
114. *Midsummer Holiday Number of Scribner's Monthly*, "The Cook of the Confederate Army," August 1879.
115. Fourth Census of the United States, 1820, NARA microfilm publication M33, 142 rolls, Records of the Bureau of the Census, Record Group 29, National Archives, Washington, D.C.
116. National Archives and Records Administration, *Index to the Compiled Military Service Records for the Volunteer Soldiers Who Served During the War of*

1812 (Washington, D.C.: National Archives and Records Administration), M602, 234 rolls.
117. *Richmond Whig*, "Whig Barbecue at Earlysville," September 17, 1844; *Richmond Dispatch*, "Elks Have a Barbecue in Albemarle," August 16, 1902.
118. Duke, *"Recollections."*
119. *Richmond Times-Dispatch*, "Important Step Taken by Masons," August 11, 1910.
120. Duke, *"Recollections."*
121. *University of Virginia Alumni News*, "Barbecue Specialists Prepare for Big Centennial Event," April 1921.
122. *Richmond Times-Dispatch*, May 7, 1946.
123. *The Times*, "How to Make Old Virginia Brunswick Stew," August 11, 1901.
124. Lyon Gardiner Tyler, ed., *Encyclopedia of Virginia Biography*, repr. ed. (Baltimore, MD: Genealogical Publishing, 1998); VMI Archives Historical Rosters, "Augustine Royall."
125. *The Times*, "How to Make Old Virginia Brunswick Stew," August 11, 1901.
126. *Richmond Times-Dispatch*, "To Give Big Brunswick Stew Picnic," September 25, 1932.
127. *Richmond Times-Dispatch*, "Post Perfects Plans for an All-Day Picnic," July 3, 1924.
128. Charles L. Perdue, ed., "Sergeant Saunders' Brunswick Stew," in *Pigsfoot Jelly & Persimmon Beer: Foodways from the Virginia Writers' Project* (Santa Fe, NM: Ancient City Press, 1992), 46–49.
129. *Richmond Times-Dispatch*, "The Art of the Stew," December 15, 1946.
130. *Richmond Times-Dispatch*, "Main Street," September 25, 1928.
131. *Jackson Sun*, March 6, 2013.
132. *Atlanta Constitution*, September 7, 1899.
133. *Richmond Times-Dispatch*, "Mrs. B.G. Fearnow Sold Her First Chicken Stew in the Early '20s; It's Been Going Since," June 19, 1955; *Richmond Times-Dispatch*, "Mrs. Fearnow, 88, Dies; Canning Firm Founder," March 7, 1970.

Chapter 6

1. *Pittsburg Daily Post*, "Kentuckians Greet Bryan," September 16, 1896.
2. *Daily Journal and Journal Tribune*, October 9, 1890.

3. *Newark Advocate*, "Rich, Savory Burgoo Plays a Part Campaign Adjunct in Kentucky," October 6, 1903.
4. *Plain Dealer*, "Burgoo," August 23, 1914.
5. William Dwight Whitney and Benjamin E. Smith, eds., *The Century Dictionary and Cyclopedia* (New York: Century Company, 1914).
6. *Lyceum Magazine* 26, no. 7, "Independent's Alert" (November 1916).
7. *Lexington Herald*, December 2, 1930.
8. *Plain Dealer*, "Burgoo," August 23, 1914.
9. G.G. Vest, "A Senator of Two Republics," *Saturday Evening Post*, January 16, 1904, 11; Eliza Leslie, *Miss Leslie's Complete Cookery Directions for Cookery, in Its Various Branches*, 34th ed. (Philadelphia, PA: Carey & Hart, 1849), 28.
10. *Alexandria Gazette*, "A Brunswick Stew," June 26, 1855.
11. Irvin S. Cobb, *Those Times and These* (New York: Review of Reviews, 1917), 313–14.
12. *Atchison Daily Globe*, September 4, 1885.
13. Alvin F. Harlow, *Weep No More, My Lady* (New York: Whittlesey House, 1942), 292; R. Gerald Alvey, "Grease Spots in the Air," in *Kentucky Bluegrass Country* (Jackson: University Press of Mississippi, 1992), 270; *Kentucky New Era*, "Burgoo Has Long History in Kentucky," April 28, 1992.
14. *San Antonio Light*, "Takes Racehorse to Let World Know of Burgoo," May 16, 1932.
15. *Daily Illinois State Register*, "Mt. Sterling's Burgoo," August 28, 1878.
16. *Fort Worth Daily Gazette*, "Burgoo Party," August 24, 1890.
17. Vest, "Senator of Two Republics," 11.
18. *Weekly Courier-Journal*, "Answers to Correspondents," November 19, 1888.
19. *Evening Public Ledger*, "'Marion Harland,' Author, 91, Dead," June 3, 1922.
20. *Evening Public Ledger*, "Burgoo," August 4, 1916.
21. Vest, "Senator of Two Republics," 11.
22. *Star News*, "Burgoo King Rebuffs Rumors," August 3, 1977.
23. *Lexington Herald*, "About Making Burgoo," May 12, 1929.
24. C.A. Rominger, *American Journal of Dental Science* 27, no. 7, "A Brunswick Stew" (May 18, 1893).
25. Marion W. Flexner, "Soups," in *Out of Kentucky Kitchens* (Lexington: University Press of Kentucky, 2010), 45.
26. *Kingsport News*, "Frenchman's Burgoo," June 29, 1872; *Fort Wayne Daily Gazette*, "Indiana and Her Neighbors," September 1, 1870.
27. *Kentucky New Era*, "Burgoo Has Long History in Kentucky," April 28, 1992.

28. Eric Partridge and Jacqueline Simpson, *The Routledge Dictionary of Historical Slang* (London: Routledge and K. Paul, 1973).
29. Leslie, *Miss Leslie's Complete Cookery Directions*, 302.
30. 702 ABC Sydney, "Last Male WWI Veteran Dies," May 5, 2011, http://www.abc.net.au/news/stories/2011/05/05/3208495.htm?site=sydney.
31. Edward Coxere, *Adventures by Sea of Edward Coxere*, ed. Edward Harry William Meyerstein (Oxford, UK: Clarendon Press, 1945).
32. Society of Gentlemen in Scotland, *Encyclopædia Britannica: Or, a Dictionary of Arts and Sciences*, vol. 1 (Edinburgh: printed for A. Bell and C. Macfarquhar, 1771), 691; *London Evening Chronicle*, "Admiralty Sessions," February 10, 1825; Thomas Trotter, *Medicina Nautica: An Essay on the Diseases of Seamen* (London: printed for T. Cadell, Jun. and W. Davies, successors to Mr. Cadell, 1797), 115. Bargou is oatmeal gruel.
33. *Boston Courier*, "City Intelligence," February 12, 1855.
34. Society of Gentlemen in Scotland, *Encyclopædia Britannica*, 797; Samuel Leech, *Thirty Years from Home* (Boston: Tappan & Dennet, 1843), 46.
35. Danske Dandridge, *American Prisoners of the Revolution* (Baltimore, MD: Genealogical Pub., 1967).
36. *Evening Post*, "Influence of Wholesome Food," August 29, 1840.
37. *Observer*, "The Young Prince and the Old Lord," November 22, 1841.
38. Mary Eaton, "Scotch Burgoo," in *The Cook and Housekeeper's Complete and Universal Dictionary* (Bungay, Suffolk: J. and R. Childs, 1823), 344.
39. M.M. Drymon, "History," in *Scotch-Irish Foodways in America: Recipes from History* (N.p.: printed by CreateSpace, 2009), 16.
40. Lauren D. Ragland, *Pioneer Index of Randolph County, West Virginia* (Bowden, WV: Seneca Pub., 2007), 2; *The Democrat*, "Notes from Webster," May 11, 1874.
41. Chapman Coleman, *The Life of John J. Crittenden, with Selections from His Correspondence and Speeches* (Philadelphia, PA: Lippincott, 1873).
42. *Richmond Climax*, "What Burgoo Really Means," October 15, 1902; *The Standard*, "Local Agents to Meet, Dine, and Orate Oct. 11," October 3, 1902.
43. *Cincinnati Post*, "Blamed the Burgoo," July 22, 1904.
44. *Lexington Herald*, "A Kentucky Burgoo-Master," November 29, 1914.
45. *Evansville Courier and Press*, June 18, 1887.
46. *Kansas City Times*, "A 'Burgout Feast,'" August 15, 1885.
47. Whitney and Smith, *Century Dictionary and Cyclopedia*, 726.
48. *The Sun*, "Irish Stew," September 24, 1909.
49. Solomon H. Katz, "Pioneer Food," in *Encyclopedia of Food and Culture* (New York: Scribner, 2003), 464.

50. *Evening Public Ledger*, "Burgoo," August 4, 1916.
51. *Evening Public Ledger*, "Recipe for Burgoo," August 16, 1916; *Daily State Journal*, "John J. Crittenden and Old Kentucky Customs," June 29, 1872; *Fort Wayne Daily Gazette*, "Burgoo," September 1, 1870.
52. *New York Times*, "What a Kentucky Burgoo Is," July 27, 1884.
53. *Lexington Herald*, "Clark Democrats Open State Campaign," July 23, 1916.
54. *M. Ligmot, Bonfort's Wine and Spirit Circular*, "Owensboro Notes," October 25, 1887.
55. *Moberly Monitor*, "Burgoo King Got His Name from a Southern Delicacy," May 16, 1932.
56. *Plain Dealer*, "Burgoo," September 30, 1894.
57. *Patriot*, "Kentucky Burgoo," May 31, 1887.
58. Daniel Carter Beard, *The American Boys' Handybook of Camp-Lore and Woodcraft* (Philadelphia, PA: J.B. Lippincott Company, 1920), 119; *The Standard*, "Local Agents to Meet, Dine, and Orate Oct. 11."
59. Dan Beard, "Good Things to Eat," *Boys' Life*, March 1925.
60. *Daily State Journal*, "John J. Crittenden and Old Kentucky Customs," June 29, 1872.
61. *Hartford (CT) Times*, "A Kentucky Barbecue," August 5, 1843.
62. *Lexington Leader*, "28,800 Cups and 35,000 Spoons," August 29, 1912.
63. *Daily Register Gazette*, "Encampment Relics," April 21, 1896; *Lexington Herald*, "Cooking as Unique as Crowd Is Great," April 25, 1907.
64. *National Tribune*, "Tribunets," October 10, 1895.
65. *Evening Bulletin*, June 26, 1885.
66. *Riverside Daily Press*, October 23, 1896.
67. *Evening Star*, "Kentucky Politics," August 16, 1898.
68. *Charleston News and Courier*, "Boss of Burgoo and Barbecue," June 3, 1906.
69. *Kansas City Star*, "Why No More Burgoo?," September 10, 1906.
70. *Plain Dealer*, "Burgoo," September 30, 1894.
71. *The Courier*, September 8, 1894.
72. *Zanesville Signal*, "What Is the Origin of Kentucky Burgoo?," December 8, 1936.
73. *Indianapolis Sun*, "Burgoo Plays a Part in Kentucky Campaign," September 25, 1903.
74. *Cook County News-Herald*, October 13, 1921.
75. *Lexington Herald*, "Noted Burgoo Maker and Wife Wedded 50 Years Ago Today," October 13, 1918.
76. *San Francisco Chronicle*, "Boone's Burgoo," October 1, 1888.

77. *New York Times*, "What a Kentucky Burgoo Is," July 27, 1884.
78. *Kingsport News*, "Kentucky in Stew Over Real Burgoo," April 20, 1948.
79. *Kingsport News*, "Frenchman's Burgoo," June 21, 1963.
80. *Oakland Tribune*, "Kentucky Burgoo Drips with History," October 1, 1969.
81. *Paducah Evening Sun*, "Kentucky's Own Is Famous Burgoo," June 29, 1906; Mann Butler, *A History of the Commonwealth of Kentucky* (Cincinnati, OH, 1834), 190; *The Epicure: A Journal of Taste* 6, no. 69, "The Burgoo" (August 1899).
82. *The Epicure* 6, no. 69, "Burgoo."
83. *Jeffersonian Democrat*, "Anecdote of Cassius M. Clay," July 8, 1859.
84. Josiah Hazen Shinn, *Pioneers and Makers of Arkansas* (Washington, D.C.: Genealogical and Historical Pub., 1908).
85. *Richmond Dispatch*, "Grand Barbecue," September 6, 1885. Squirrel soup served at Virginia barbecues.
86. B.J. Radford, *History of Woodford County* (Peoria, IL: W.T. Dowdall, Printer, 1877), 87–88.
87. Geo Hayden, "An Illinois Burgoo," *Recreation* 6, no. 6 (June 1897).
88. *Springfield Republican*, August 21, 1871.
89. *Kingsport News*, "Kentucky in Stew Over Real Burgoo."
90. *Denver Post*, "Cattle for the Banquet," February 11, 1903.
91 *Richmond Times-Dispatch*, November 29, 1956.
92. *Fort Worth Daily Gazette*, "Burgoo Party," August 24, 1890.
93. *Daily Illinois State Register*, "The Annual Burgoo," October 19, 1894.
94. *Kansas City Times*, "Another Burgoo Feast to Be Held," August 29, 1885.
95. *St. Louis Republic*, "Mizzourah Burgoo," April 29, 1900.
96. *Kansas City Times*, "Another Burgoo Feast to Be Held."
97. *Kansas City Star*, "Why No More Burgoo?"
98. Hayden, "Illinois Burgoo."
99. Arenzville, IL—Home of the World's Best Burgoo, "What Is Burgoo?," July 31, 2013, http://www.burgoo.org/burgoo/burgoo.html.
100. *Saturday Evening Post*, "Soup-Crazy Town—Winchester, Illinois," August 8, 1953.
101. Samantha McDaniel-Ogletree, "Community Picnic Revived, Helps Restore Pride," *The Telegraph*, July 19, 2014, http://www.thetelegraph.com/news/home_top-news/31228894/Community-picnic-revived-helps-restore-pride.
102. *Bourbon News*, "Famous Burgoo Maker Dies at Lexington," April 2, 1920.
103. *Charleston News and Courier*, "Boss of Burgoo and Barbecue," June 3, 1906.

104. *Paducah Evening Sun*, "Kentucky's Own Is Famous Burgoo," June 29, 1906; *Louisville Courier-Journal*, "The Kentucky Barbecue," November 7, 1897; *Lincoln Daily News*, "Famous Kentucky Cook," December 11, 1914.
105. *American Magazine*, "The Kentucky Burgoo Master" (December 1914): 64.
106. *The Sun*, "Boss of Burgoo and Barbecue," June 3, 1906.
107. *Lexington Herald*, "Noted Burgoo Maker and Wife."
108. Edwin Carty Ranck, "A Kentucky Burgoo-Master," *American Magazine* (December 1914); *Lexington Herald*, "A Kentucky Burgoo-Master."
109. *Kingsport News*, "Kentucky in Stew Over Real Burgoo."
110. *Burlington Weekly Free Press*, "Famous Cook Who Has Fed 200,000 in a Day," December 3, 1914.
111. *Paducah Evening Sun*, "Kentucky's Own Is Famous Burgoo," June 29, 1906.
112. *Kingsport News*, "Kentucky in Stew Over Real Burgoo."
113. *Lexington Leader*, "Burgoo King," July 17, 1904.
114. *The Sun*, "Boss of Burgoo and Barbecue," June 3, 1906; *Lexington Leader*, January 18, 1893.
115. *Newark Advocate*, "Rich, Savory Burgoo Plays a Part Campaign Adjunct in Kentucky," October 6, 1903; *Louisville Courier-Journal*, "The Kentucky Barbecue," November 7, 1897.
116. *Hickman Courier*, "An Interesting Relic," June 21, 1907; *Lincoln Daily News*, "Famous Kentucky Cook," December 11, 1914; *Lexington Herald*, "Noted Burgoo Maker and Wife."
117. *American Magazine*, "Kentucky Burgoo Master," 64.
118. *Newark Advocate*, "Rich, Savory Burgoo Plays a Part Campaign Adjunct in Kentucky," October 6, 1903.
119. *Louisville Courier-Journal*, "The Kentucky Barbecue," November 7, 1897.
120. *Centralia Enterprise and Tribune*, "Burgoo Galore," September 7, 1895.
121. Pere Marquette Railway, New York, C. & St. Louis Railroad, Chesapeake and Ohio Railway Company, *Tracks: Chesapeake & Ohio, Nickel Plate, Pere Marquette*, vol. 31, no. 6 (New York: Geffen, Dunn & Company 1946).
122. *Roanoke Times*, "Grand Army of the Republic," September 14, 1895; *American Magazine*, "Kentucky Burgoo Master." This resource claims that Jaubert fed 200,000 people.
123. *American Magazine*, "Kentucky Burgoo Master," 64; *Chronicle*, "Our American Letter," November 23, 1895.
124. *The Sun*, "Boss of Burgoo and Barbecue," June 3, 1906.
125. *Chronicle*, "Our American Letter," November 23, 1895.

126. *San Francisco Chronicle*, "Boone's Burgoo," October 1, 1888.
127. *Lincoln Daily News*, "Famous Kentucky Cook," December 11, 1914.
128. Family History Library, Year: 1870; Census Place: Lexington Ward 2, Fayette, Kentucky; Roll: M593_460; Page: 198A; Image: 403; Family History Library Film: 545959.
129. *Lexington Herald*, "Cooking as Unique as Crowd Is Great."
130. *Morning Herald*, August 21, 1898.
131. *Morning Herald*, June 19, 1903.
132. *The Sun*, "Boss of Burgoo and Barbecue," June 3, 1906.
133. *Lexington Herald*, "Noted Burgoo Maker and Wife."
134. *Lexington Herald*, "In Memory of Gus Jaubert," March 30, 1920.
135. *Lexington Leader*, January 18, 1893.
136. *Lexington Herald*, "Noted Burgoo Maker and Wife." Although the newspaper author claimed that Jaubert's last barbecue and burgoo was cooked for Senator Camden in 1914, based on newspaper articles published about Camden's barbecues in 1913 and 1914, the last account of one held by Camden at Spring Hill that mentions Gus Jaubert occurred in 1913. In 1914, the Camden barbecue was cooked by Dud Lawrence.
137. *Jacksonville Daily Journal*, "Gus Jaubert Champion Soup Maker of Kentucky," December 1, 1914.
138. *Lexington Herald*, "About Making Burgoo," May 12, 1929.
139. The 1880 federal census lists the occupations of Watson Green; his wife, Susan; and his oldest daughter, Ella, as "cook."
140. *Courier-Journal*, "The Turf," May 9, 1876.
141. *Lexington Leader*, February 18, 1914; Kentucky Department for Libraries and Archives, *Vital Statistics Original Death Certificates—Microfilm (1911–1955)*, Microfilm rolls #7016130-7041803, Kentucky Department for Libraries and Archives, Frankfort, Kentucky. There are conflicting records of Riggs's age at the time of his death. His newspaper obituary claims that he was eighty-seven years old when he died and had worked with Gus Jaubert for thirty-five years. However, the only death certificate that can be found for an Aaron Riggs who died in the Shelby, Kentucky area in March 1914 indicates that he was fifty-four years of age when he died.
142. Karen Hess, *The Carolina Rice Kitchen: The African Connection* (Columbia: University of South Carolina Press, 1992).
143. *Cincinnati Enquirer*, "Tongues of Prize Orators," August 27, 1916.
144. *Lexington Leader*, "'Dud' Lawrence," May 30, 1909; *Lexington Herald*, "Kentucky Barbecue for Winchester Democrats," August 20, 1916.

145. *Lexington Leader*, "Camden Barbecue," August 21, 1913; *Lexington Herald*, "Everything Is Ready for Great Barbecue Camden Gives Today," August 30, 1913.
146. *Lexington Herald*, "Co-Operation Urged by All Speakers at Woodford Barbecue," July 29, 1914.
147. *Lexington Leader*, "'Dud' Lawrence Dies After Long Illness," September 12, 1931; *Lexington Leader*, "Making Burgoo in Boston," May 17, 1904; *Lexington Leader*, "To Make Burgoo for Harvard Alumni," May 24, 1929; *Lexington Leader*, "Dud Lawrence Tells of Republican Rally," September 24, 1915.
148. *New York Tribune*, "Crowd of 40,000 Eat Burgoo and Cheer Harding's Speech," October 21, 1920.
149. *Lexington Herald*, "Former Lexingtonian Dies at Race Track," July 7, 1954.
150. *Lexington Herald*, "'Burgoo King' Looney, 84, Dies After Brief Illness," March 24, 1954.
151. *Edwardsville Intelligencer*, "What Is Burgoo?," July 9, 1958.
152. *National Labor Tribune*, "The 'Burgoo King' Does His Stuff," July 7, 1932.
153. *San Antonio Light*, "Takes Racehorse to Let World Know of Burgoo," May 16, 1932.
154. *Kingsport News*, "Kentucky in Stew Over Real Burgoo."
155. Ibid.
156. Raymond A. Sokolov, "A Squirrel in Every Pot: Brunswick Stew and Burgoo," in *Fading Feast: A Compendium of Disappearing American Regional Foods* (New York: Farrar Straus Giroux, 1981), 79.
157. *Kokomo Tribune*, "Answers to Questions," December 14, 1936.
158. *Moberly Monitor-Index*, "Burgoo King Got His Name from a Southern Delicacy," May 16, 1932.
159. Thomas Affleck, ed., *The Western Farmer and Gardener*, vols. 2–3 (Cincinnati, OH: Charles Foster, 1841), 174. In 1841, a racehorse named Burgout was three years old.
160. *National Republican*, "Baltimore Races," May 28, 1875; *National Republican*, "The Races at Bennings," May 20, 1876; *New York Herald*, "Racing at Washington," November 2, 1876; *New York Herald*, August 28 1875.
161. Beard, *Jack of All Trades*; *Dallas Morning News*, "Boy Scout Head Gives Directions on Burgoo Making," August 25, 1933.
162. *Jacksonville Journal Courier*, "Elza Perry to Celebrate 95th Birthday," July 2, 1972.
163. *Jacksonville Daily Journal*, "Burgoo King at Arenzville Homecoming," September 6, 1953.

Chapter 7

1. *Lexington Herald*, "Man Falls Headlong into Boiling Burgoo," August 15, 1913; *Lexington Herald*, "Negro Scalded in Burgoo Kettle Dies," August 16, 1913; *Columbus Daily Enquirer*, "Picnicker Falls into Burgoo Pot; Stewed," August 16, 1913.
2. *Kingsport News*, "Kentucky in Stew Over Real Burgoo."
3. *Index Journal*, "Recipe for Southern Barbecue Hash, Meat," June 22, 1959.

INDEX

A

Anburey, Thomas 41
arepas 46
Arthur, Margaret 64
Assiniboine 16

B

Bacheller, Irvin 59
Bagby, George W. 35
baking hoe 43
barbecue clubs 30
barbecue hash
  in Georgia 69
  in Pennsylvania 71
  in South Carolina 72
  in Virginia 67, 68, 70
  Lowcountry 74, 152
  redolent of onions 66
  string 74
  Upcountry 72, 152

Benton, J.M. 123
Beverly, Robert 34
bird stew 124
Boone, Daniel 132
Boyle, W.H. 83
Bradbury, John 51
bread hoe 42, 43
Brunswick stew
  a farmer's stew 60
  at Fort Christianna 96
  "church-builder chicken" 78
  during the Civil War 93
  from squirrel soup 57
  in Appalachia 79
  in California 79
  in Florida 79
  in Georgia 79, 87
  in Jamestown, Virginia 96
  in Kentucky 79
  in Michigan 79
  in North Carolina 79
  in Paris, France 81
  made with dog meat 93

INDEX

proclamations and resolutions 94
squirrel soup 33
Stockdell's Genuine Georgia 116
Sturdivant's Old Virginia–Style 114
Brunswick stew letters 103, 107, 114
"Brunswick stew letters, the" 98
Bryan, Lettice 70
burgoo
  "beergood" 127
  burbon ragout 127
  burghul 124
  "burgood" 127
  club 129
  during Revolutionary War 125
  in Illinois 135, 136
  in Missouri 135
  in Ohio 135
  in Virginia 135
  Kentucky Brunswick stew 120
  loblolly 125
  mystical powers 131
  nautical 125
  Scotch burgoo 126
  skillagallee 125
  song 130
  squirrel soup 58, 60, 135
Burgoo Committee 128
Burgoo Creek 126

C

Camden, Johnson N. 141
Caroline of Brunswick 103
chicken muddle 97
Choules, Claude 125
Clayton, John 34

Cobb, Irvin S. 120
Corbaley, Samuel 60
corn
  grated 85
  kernals scraped off cob 85
  split kernals 85
  thickens Brunswick stew 85
corn muddle 86
Cresswell, Nicholas 35
Cridlin, Chiles 155
Crisp, John T. 135, 136
Crittenden, John J. 126
Crook, William H. 53

D

Davis, Andrew Jack 116
Davis, Anne Stone 116
De Smet, Pierre-Jean 67
Duke, Richard Thomas Walker, Jr. 15, 31, 33, 108
Duke, Richard Thomas Walker, Sr. 15, 31, 83, 108
Dundas sheep stew 21
Dunlap, William 47

E

Edlin, Abraham 42
Eggleston, Edward 43
Ellis, James Tandy 124
Estes, J.A. 59

F

Farm Life Stew Crew 105

INDEX

Fishwick, Marshall 34
Fithian, Philip Vickers 37
Flexner, Marion 124
Fort Christianna 100
Frost, Roon 47
frybread 46
Fulton, Captain Andrew 52

G

Garfield, James A. 54
Garth, Juba 31
Garth, Mandy 31
Gillete, Fanny Lemira 49
Gilmore, John 110
Gist, Nat 147
Godman, John Davidson 51
gray squirrel 50
"Great Brunswick Stew
    Controversy, the" 90, 91, 92,
    93, 94, 98
Griffin, Thomas 104
Gwaltney, P.D., Jr. 37

H

Haislip, William 75
Harland, Marion 43, 58, 77, 122, 128
hash
  definition 62, 64
  during Civil War 63
  during World War II 72
  giblet 67, 69
  hidden 64, 68
  liver 67
  Native Americans 67
  Rocky Mountain 67

Haskins, Creed 102, 105, 107
Hearne, Robert J. 127
Heartwell, Horace Hilliard 95
Hess, Karen 44
Hobbs, Richard 61
Hobgood, Alfred 68
hoecake 41, 149
hogs
  in Virginia 34
  "Virginia rabbits" 34
Homes, Colonel 96

J

Jackson, Stonewall 56
Jaubert, Gus 123, 124, 130, 132,
    137
johnnycakes 45
Jones, Hugh 34
journey cakes 45

K

kedjenou 17
Kellum, Anne Davis 116
Kieth, Amos 127
kissing soup parties 56

L

Lawrence, Nelson Dudley 143
Lea, Elizabeth Ellicot 42
Lee, Robert E. 53
Looney, James T. 144

Index

M

Mason, Bell K. 103
Mason, John Y. 81
Mason, William Thomas 102
Matthews, James ("Uncle Jimmy") 83, 100, 102, 107
  in the War of 1812 102
McConnaughey, Gibson Jefferson 33
McKinley, William 76
Moore, Carrie Pickett 84
Morgan, John Hunt 133
msíckquatash 18

N

nixtamalization 47
nocake 45
Norris, Thaddeus 32

O

offal 21, 63

P

Paschall, Elizabeth Coates 71
Patawomeck 18
Proclamation Stew Crew 155

R

Randolph, Mary 69
recipes
  Kentucky Colonel Burgoo 149
  Old Virginia Brunswick Stew 148
  South Carolina–Style Barbecue Hash 150
  Virginia Hoecakes 154
  Virginia-Style Barbecued Pork 153
  Virginia-Style Barbecue Hash 153
  Virginia-Style Barbecue Sauce 152
  Virginia-Style Brunswick Stew Recipes for Large Batches 155
Riggs, Aaron 142
rockahomin 47
Royall, Augustine 96

S

Scotch burgoo 128
Scotch-Irish 127
Scott, Early 30
Severance, Sam 132
Shouse, Jouette 135
Sinclair, Upton 75
Smith, James 67
Smith, John 42, 46, 80
sops 17
spoon-meat 62
spoons 61
Spotswood, Governor 96
Sprigg, James Cresap 95
squirrels
  in California 51
  in Ohio 52
  in Pennsylvania 52
  in the United States 50

Index

  in Virginia 50, 52, 57
  medicinal powers 53
squirrel scalps 52, 53
Steed, Bill 105
Steed, Chad 105
Stith, Jack 102
Stith, Ned 100, 102, 103, 137
Stone Boilers 16

T

Taft, President 87
tamales 41, 46
Tar Heel letter 100, 103, 107
Terhune, Mary Virginia 77
tortillas 46
Trumbull, James Hammond 45
tuckahoe 43, 45
Tuckahoes (Tidewater Virginians) 45
Tyree, Marion Cabell 84

V

Vest, George Graham 122, 135
Virginia
  Barbecue Season 27, 28
  soups (events) 55
  the "trinity" 78, 103
  truffle 45

W

Wesley, John 90
Whitlow, Jackson 54
Williams, Roger 45
Wood, William 45
WPA soup 18

Z

Zimmern, Andrew 25

ABOUT THE AUTHOR

Born in Virginia, Joseph Ray Haynes has lived in the state his entire life. Through his father, his family tree reaches back in Virginia to colonial times. Through his mother, he is a descendent of the Patawomeck Indian tribe of Virginia. Joe's love of Brunswick stew grew out of the version of the stew cooked by his mother. Every year, his father grew an abundance of vegetables, including the butterbeans, tomatoes, corn and potatoes that are important ingredients in real Virginia-style Brunswick stew. His father also raised chickens, cattle and hogs in addition to being an avid hunter of deer, dove and squirrels. On many occasions, his mother expertly prepared delicious pots of stew using those ingredients to serve to her family.

Over the years, Joe was tutored by some of the best Brunswick stew cooks in Virginia and has himself cooked his share of Brunswick stew for fundraisers and community events outdoors in large iron kettles. He is an award-winning competition barbecue cook, and the world's largest organization of barbecue enthusiasts has certified him as a master barbecue judge. In 2012, he was the recipient of the Leadership in Barbecue Award given by the organizers of the annual BBQ Jamboree in Fredericksburg, Virginia.

In addition to this book, Joe also authored *Virginia Barbecue: A History*, published by The History Press, and the Virginia Barbecue Proclamation that unanimously passed as a House Joint Resolution in 2016 wherein it states, "Resolved by the House of Delegates, the Senate concurring, that the General Assembly designate May through October, in 2016 and in each succeeding year, as Virginia's official Barbecue Season."

Visit us at
www.historypress.net

This title is also available as an e-book